Homestyle
Family Favorites
Annual Recipes ■ *2009*

Classic Potluck Dishes

Francine Halvorsen

RODALE

Portions of this book were previously published as *Crowd-Pleasing Potluck* (© Francine Halvorsen, 2007)

Printed in the United States of America
Rodale Inc. makes every effort to use acid-free ♾, recycled paper ♻.

Photographs by © Mitch Mandel/Rodale Images
Food Styling by Dan Macey

Book design by Christina Gaugler

ISBN-13   978–1–60529–887–0
ISBN-10   1–60529–887–5

2   4   6   8   10   9   7   5   3   1   hardcover

For "the kids"—Benjamin, Emilia, Harrison, Isaiah, Jacob, Megan, and Sarah—with love and laughter. You grace any meal with your presence.

ACKNOWLEDGMENTS

With thanks from A to Z to Pamela Adler and Claire Zuckerman for being there, to Jesse Halvorsen; Linda Lee; Lionel Halvorsen; Gail and Barry Cohen; Carol Weaver; Felix Harlan; Susan Lewis; and Elizabeth, Alan, and Song Lee for confirming continuously that food tastes only as good as the people you share it with.

With thanks to the team at Rodale, most especially my editor Karen Bolesta, who has been skillful and good-natured through thick and thin, and Shea Zukowski who shepherded the book from its early stages. Copy editors Rachelle Laliberte and Ellen Bingham kept many a slip from showing and Tara Long and Diane Meckel made order out of chaos, while Lois Hazel kept everything on track. Dan Macey and Melissa Reiss, working with photographer Mitch Mandel, made sure that the food looks good enough to eat. I appreciate all your time, talent, and enthusiasm.

A special word of gratitude to the Thursday Taizé meditation and potluck group at the Cathedral of the Incarnation in Baltimore. Thank you all.

CONTENTS

INTRODUCTION

I ONCE CARRIED A HAM, A TURKEY, and stuffing on a flight from New York to Chicago. My mom was unexpectedly ill and could not travel so we decided to celebrate the holiday at her house. Since I was the one most unflappable about presenting food in a variety of circumstances, I was designated to do the lion's share of cooking and assembling the 'pre-fab' meal. Happily, it turned out to be 'fab.' The secret—dishes that travel well and a very well-insulated thermal bag with lots of cold packs. Though I am sure hams and turkeys are no longer allowable carry-ons, there are almost no limitations to potluck.

THE ART OF POTLUCKING

I never thought that what my friends and family were doing was potluck. We seem much too contemporary and too much into good food, and we have professional and private lives that keep us busy. I was talking to a friend who said she never 'does' pot-lucks. I asked, well what do you call it when you want to get 10 or 12 people together and you ask me to bring dessert, Liz to please bring the great salad she makes, and Adam to bring some cheese and those spicy olives he mixes. She said, "Oh."

At this point I don't think I know anyone who has not been asked to bring something to eat somewhere where other people will share it. That's what potluck is—*a meal at which each guest brings food that is then shared by all.* More and more private and professional events are staged by family and friends with busy lives. These people, who love to cook and give parties but have time to do only one or two dishes really well, will ask others to bring something.

From casual dinners and holidays, to public celebrations and occasions too numerous and varied to list, from studio apartments and commodious houses to conference rooms and gardens, people are sharing the art of potlucking. In cities and in suburbs, everyone is bringing something to the table.

When the burden of an entire meal is lifted, the tasks of shopping, organizing, cooking and serving are simplified and you can focus your attention on a great recipe. Usually a dish can be served "as brought" or needs only to be heated, dressed, and plated. Sometimes a dish you decide to cook may require some assembly and finishing. Tips I've learned from experience and from interviews with chefs and caterers will enable you to prepare and present top-notch dishes that will have people asking for your recipe.

With the recipes and suggestions in this book you get the opportunity to show off your specialty and get ideas for new ones. The range of dishes are delicious but none require elaborate last-minute preparations. Planning is as important as your unique seasoning.

Food is both a kindness to others and an instant reward for ourselves. Those "oohs" and "aahs" are very gratifying. Whether you are bringing salad or dessert to a family dinner for eight people or two 12-inch by 20-inch sheet cakes to provide many people with a little something to go with their coffee, it is a nice feeling to shine.

You might think that many people cooking for one occasion would cause inconsistencies, but what I have discovered as I have participated in hundreds of potlucks over the years in this country and others, is that a certain harmonious composition occurs. Everyone enjoys bringing a dish and everyone enjoys eating something made by someone else. Don't underestimate your group. The Mediterranean Stuffed Peppers with the chopped pistachios and fresh mint will be as much appreciated at your congregation's after-service get together as it was at your book club meeting.

The best meals are composed of established crowd-pleasers and a few new dishes. All the recipes in the main section of the book serve 8 to 12 and almost all of them can be halved or multiplied. Most markets have all the items that you will need; some elements will require special shopping, and a few can be made from ingredients found in a convenience store.

That being said, always use the freshest best ingredients that you can get. Omit tomatoes if they feel like wax candles—they will probably taste like wax candles. I once interviewed the executive chef of the Excelsior Hotel on the Via Veneto in Rome and after showing me some remarkably elaborate dishes, we went into the cavernous kitchen. Among other questions, I asked him what he did when there were no ripe tomatoes. In less than fifteen minutes a chef made me a tomato sauce from drained, canned peeled tomatoes, pancetta, and broccoli rabe, and pasta from a box. The secret ingredient to good cooking is flexibility. Often the simplest dishes seem the most luxurious.

I hope that, as with all really useful guides, this book's attention to detail will free you to be confident and creative as you prepare your dishes. Anyone, from the seasoned pro to the enthusiastic home cook, can follow these recipes. All the practical considerations are covered, but most are common sense, and stress-free.

Give it your best shot. The food made from *Classic Potluck Dishes* will be delicious and much appreciated. Shared occasions are people events first and eating events second, which is why "the art of potlucking" is always a joy and your contribution always welcome.

—*Francine Halvorsen*

HORS D'OEUVRES AND APPETIZERS

NOT ONLY ARE THE RECIPES IN THIS CHAPTER excellent starters, but these recipes in various combinations—especially when paired with fruit, sweets, and beverages—make more than enough food for many gatherings.

Most of the selections included are very forgiving. The French names give you the right idea—*hors d'oeuvres* means "out of the work"; *amuse-bouche* translates as "to amuse the mouth." Many of these recipes can be made a day or more before they are needed. If you are uncertain about serving supplies at your destination, bring along some small or medium durable paper or plastic plates (most people enjoy grazing with small plates), forks and spreaders, and plenty of napkins. Individually packaged wet towels are not necessary but are very welcome.

If you are hosting an event, ask whoever is bringing starters to come a bit early so people can enjoy them when they arrive.

Seville-Style Olives (opposite)
Spicy Black Olives with Garlic and Herbs (page 4)
Ginger-Roasted Almonds (page 5)
Spicy Pecans (page 6)

SEVILLE-STYLE OLIVES

Try to use Spanish olives for this recipe; they are known for their unique flavor and texture. And if you can find Spanish olive oil as well, it will give an authentic touch. You can use any large green olive and get delicious results.

YIELD | 2 CUPS

1	pound large green Spanish olives
¼	cup extra-virgin olive oil
¼	cup sherry vinegar
6	anchovy fillets, minced
6	cloves garlic, peeled and crushed

1	tablespoon minced fresh thyme or ½ tablespoon dried
1	teaspoon crushed red pepper flakes
4	bay leaves

Place the olives in a large bowl and bruise them with the back of a wooden spoon. Add all the other ingredients and stir. Divide the mixture between two 1-pint glass canning jars or any jars with tight-fitting lids. Marinate in the refrigerator for a week. They will keep in the refrigerator for up to 2 weeks.

To serve the dish: These olives are best served at room temperature. Be sure to remove any pieces of bay leaf before serving.

SPICY BLACK OLIVES WITH GARLIC AND HERBS

YIELD | APPROXIMATELY 2 CUPS

1	pound black olives	4	sprigs fresh thyme and/or rosemary
3	cloves garlic, minced		Olive oil
2	small jalepeño (or your choice) chili peppers, halved lengthwise and seeded		

In a large bowl, stir together the olives and garlic. Layer them in a 1-quart glass jar with a tight-fitting lid, interspersing the peppers and herbs. Add oil to cover. Secure the lid and refrigerate for up to 2 weeks.

To serve the dish: You can place the olives in a bowl and provide a small spoon so people can help themselves to as many as they want on their plate, or you can arrange the olives on a platter and set out toothpicks. Either way, remember to provide little bowls for the discarded pits and picks.

GINGER-ROASTED ALMONDS

YIELD | 4 CUPS

1	pound (4 cups) blanched whole almonds
½	cup packed brown sugar
1	teaspoon coarse salt

2	teaspoons ground ginger
2	tablespoons honey
2	tablespoons safflower oil

Preheat the oven to 350°F.

Toast the nuts on two foil- or parchment-lined baking sheets for 5 minutes. Turn the nuts with a spatula once.

Blend the sugar, salt, ginger, honey, and oil in a small saucepan. Place over low heat and stir until the mixture is just simmering and the sugar is dissolved, 3 to 5 minutes.

Remove the baking sheets from the oven, lower the heat to 325°F, and pour the honey mixture over the warm nuts. Stir and roast for an additional 10 minutes. Turn with a spatula after 2 minutes.

Remove the nuts from the baking sheets and drain on wire cake racks placed over paper towels to catch any dripping.

When the nuts are cool and dry, they can be stored in an airtight container for up to a week.

To serve the dish: Serve the nuts at room temperature.

SPICY PECANS

4	tablespoons butter, melted		A few dashes of hot pepper sauce (optional)
2	tablespoons Worcestershire sauce	1	pound (4 cups) shelled pecan halves
1	teaspoon chili powder		
1	teaspoon salt		
¼	teaspoon cayenne pepper		

Preheat the oven to 300°F.

In a large bowl, mix all the ingredients. Roast on two or three baking sheets until the pecans are aromatic and dark but not burnt, about 20 minutes.

Remove to paper towels to cool. When cooled, the seasoned pecans can be stored in an airtight container for a week.

To serve the dish: Serve at room temperature.

HOMEMADE HUMMUS

Why make your own hummus rather than buy it? Two reasons: freshness of the ingredients and texture. It is the coarseness and blandness of the chickpeas against the tang of lemon and mint that makes this recipe special.

YIELD | 4 CUPS

3	cups cooked or canned chickpeas, rinsed and drained	3	tablespoons minced fresh parsley + sprigs for garnish
1½	cups tahini	2	tablespoons minced fresh mint + sprigs for garnish
⅔	cup extra-virgin olive oil		Harissa or crushed red pepper flakes for garnish (optional)
½	cup water		
	Juice of 2 lemons		
	Salt and pepper to taste		

In a medium bowl, mash the chickpeas with a potato masher or fork and set aside.

In a bowl large enough to hold all the ingredients, blend vigorously with a fork the tahini, oil, water, lemon juice, and salt and black pepper to taste, and stir until creamy. Add the chickpeas and blend, then stir in the minced parsley and mint. If you want to make this a day or two ahead of time, omit the parsley and mint and add them before serving. The hummus can be stored, covered, in the refrigerator for 2 days. Bring to room temperature, place in a serving bowl, and stir in the minced parsley and mint.

To serve the dish: Just before serving, garnish the hummus with the mint and parsley sprigs and, if desired, harissa or red pepper flakes. Serve at room temperature along with warm pita triangles or toasts and/or lettuce leaves to scoop up the dip. The dish can be plated as a salad or served buffet-style with little plates or napkins.

POTLUCK NOTE | *Tahini, a Middle Eastern sesame paste, is widely available. Harissa is a Middle Eastern hot-pepper sauce sold at many specialty stores. If you can't find it, substitute a few pinches of red pepper flakes.*

CHICKEN SATAY SKEWERS

This peanut sauce is popular throughout Indonesia and has been adapted for many dishes.

YIELD | 20 SKEWERS

1½	cups vegetable or chicken stock	⅓	cup chopped fresh cilantro
1½	cups crunchy peanut butter	3	scallions, chopped
2	cloves garlic, minced	2	limes, thinly sliced, for garnish
2	teaspoons chili powder	1	cup unsalted roasted peanuts, chopped, for garnish
½	cup hoisin sauce or light soy sauce		
¼	cup packed brown sugar		
5	skinless, boneless chicken breast halves, cut into 20 strips		

In a medium saucepan over medium heat, combine the stock, peanut butter, garlic, chili powder, hoisin or soy sauce, and sugar. Cook, stirring, until thoroughly blended, 5 to 7 minutes. Stir well and set aside 1½ cups.

Place the remaining sauce in a shallow dish and add the chicken strips. Cover and refrigerate for at least 2 hours or overnight. While the chicken is marinating, soak twenty 10- to 12-inch bamboo skewers in water for 1 hour so they will not burn on the grill.

Add the cilantro and scallions to the reserved 1½ cups satay sauce. *Never cross-contaminate by using marinade that has had contact with raw food as part of any sauce.* Thread 1 chicken strip onto each skewer. If you're not serving right away, wrap the skewered chicken in plastic, cover the sauce, and carry to your destination in a cooler bag.

To broil the satay skewers, wrap any visible wood in aluminum foil and place on a broiling pan 6 inches under the hot oven broiler. Cook, turning once, until the chicken is no longer pink, 8 to 10 minutes. Place on a platter and remove the foil.

To serve the dish: If you have a portable grill, such as a George Foreman, bring it with you and grill the skewers for 5 to 7 minutes per side about 20 minutes before serving. On an outdoor grill, cook the skewers over hot coals, turning once, until the chicken is thoroughly cooked, 6 to 8 minutes. Garnish with the lime slices and peanuts, and serve the satay dipping sauce in a bowl alongside.

ROASTED EGGPLANT DIP (BABA GHANOUSH)

Versions of this dish are found throughout the Mediterranean. Don't be too fussy when you make it; bits of charred eggplant skin, pockets of garlic, and bursts of pomegranate seeds only enhance the dip's flavor and texture.

YIELD | 4 CUPS

4	large eggplants	1	teaspoon cumin
½–¾	cup extra-virgin olive oil + more for preparing vegetables	1	teaspoon coarse salt
2	green bell peppers	¼	teaspoon black pepper
1	cup tahini		Seeds of one pomegranate (optional)
3	cloves garlic		

Preheat the broiler or the oven to 350°F.

If using the broiler, set the eggplants on foil-lined baking sheets 6 inches under the heat source, turning regularly to char the skin all over, until the eggplants become soft and deflate, about 20 minutes. If using the oven, halve the eggplants lengthwise, rub all over with oil, and place cut side down on foil-lined baking sheets. Bake for 45 minutes. When cool enough to handle, scrape the pulp from the skins into a large bowl. (If some of the charred bits get into the bowl, so much the better.) Discard the skins.

Char the bell peppers in the same manner, baking until the skin is blackened. Remove the peppers from the oven and place them in a paper bag (with the open end twisted shut) for several minutes so the steam can loosen the skins. Remove and discard the skins. Place the bell peppers in the bowl with the eggplant and chop until minced. Stir in the tahini.

Using a garlic press, squeeze the garlic cloves into a small bowl and discard the fibers that do not go through. Mix in ½ cup of the oil, cumin, salt, and black pepper, then stir into the eggplant and peppers. Cover and chill in the refrigerator until ready to serve. This can be refrigerated for 24 hours. If it is thick when you take it out of the refrigerator, add up to ¼ cup of the remaining olive oil.

To serve the dish: This dip is best served at room temperature. If desired, garnish with pomegranate seeds just before serving with Crispy Pita Chips (page 14).

TAPENADE

The quality of your olives is key to the flavor of this rich spread from the Mediterranean.

YIELD | 2 CUPS

1	pound good-quality pitted black olives	½	cup extra-virgin olive oil
¼	cup salt-cured or in-brine capers, rinsed thoroughly and drained	½	teaspoon herbes de Provence
1	can (2 ounces) flat anchovies, rinsed and drained		Juice of ½ lemon

Place the olives, capers, and anchovies in a blender and coarsely puree until somewhere between the texture of smooth peanut butter and crunchy. Remove to a bowl with the aid of a rubber spatula. Using a small hand whisk or fork, whisk in the oil, herbes de Provence, and lemon juice. Place the tapenade in a tightly sealed container and refrigerate for up to 1 week.

To serve the dish: Serve at room temperature as a spread for crackers or Crostini (below).

CROSTINI

These thin, crispy little toasts provide the perfect base for a variety of toppings, including Tapenade (above), sliced roasted tomato and basil, blue cheese and honey, or Brie and chutney.

YIELD | APPROXIMATELY 40 CROSTINI

2	baguettes (12–14 ounces each)	½	teaspoon coarse salt
½	cup olive oil		

Preheat the oven to 350°F.

Cut the bread into ½-inch-thick slices. Arrange the slices in a single layer on two ungreased baking sheets. Brush with some of the oil and sprinkle with the salt. Bake until the edges are golden brown, about 5 minutes. Brush with the remaining oil and place under the broiler for 1 to 2 minutes, then turn and broil for 1 minute longer.

BAKED BUFFALO CHICKEN WINGS

These wings are not for every event, but if you know your crowd, supply tons of napkins, a place to discard the bones, and have fun!

YIELD | 15 TO 20 SERVINGS

5 pounds (about 30) chicken wings, cut in half at the joint, wing tips removed

⅓ cup canola oil

1 teaspoon salt + more to taste

¼ teaspoon cayenne pepper (optional)

3–6 tablespoons Tabasco

1 cup mayonnaise

8 ounces (1 cup) sour cream

16 ounces (about 2 cups) blue cheese, crumbled

2 tablespoons white vinegar

¼ teaspoon freshly ground black pepper + more to taste

1–2 large heads celery, strings removed, ribs cut into 3-inch sticks, for serving

Preheat the oven to 425°F.

In a large bowl, combine the wings, oil, the 1 teaspoon salt, cayenne, and 3 to 5 tablespoons of the Tabasco. Arrange the wings in a single layer on two large rimmed baking sheets. Bake until just done, about 35 minutes. Drain on paper towels.

In a medium bowl, combine the mayonnaise, sour cream, blue cheese, vinegar, the ¼ teaspoon black pepper, and up to 1 tablespoon of the remaining Tabasco to taste. Season with salt and black pepper to taste. Cover and refrigerate for up to 24 hours.

To serve the dish: Serve the wings hot and the blue cheese dip at room temperature. If you like, you can make the marinade for the wings a day ahead and refrigerate it. Then you have the choice of making the wings at home and carrying them in a thermal container or preparing them at your destination, along with the celery sticks and blue cheese dip.

POTLUCK NOTE | *Various companies package boneless chicken wings, which make a somewhat less messy version of this dish, but they are not available in every market yet.*

CREAMY BLUE-CHEESE SPREAD

This is not the place to use fancy blue cheeses such as Humboldt Fog or Stilton, which should be served on a cheese platter. Find a reasonably priced blue and you will have a very satisfactory dip.

YIELD | 2½ CUPS

8	ounces (about 1 cup) blue cheese, at room temperature, crumbled	8	ounces (1 cup) plain yogurt
			Dash of hot sauce (optional)
4	ounces (½ cup) cream cheese, at room temperature	2	cups finely chopped fresh watercress

Place the blue cheese, cream cheese, yogurt, and hot sauce (if desired) in a large bowl and blend with a handheld electric mixer. Stir in the watercress. Cover with plastic wrap and refrigerate for up to 24 hours.

To serve the dish: Serve at room temperature.

CRISPY PITA CHIPS

YIELD | 6 DOZEN TRIANGLES

6	pitas	¼	cup olive oil

Preheat the oven to 360°F.

Cut each pita into six wedges, and separate each wedge into two at the fold.

Place the pita pieces rough side up on baking sheets and brush with the oil. Bake until lightly browned, about 8 minutes. You may want to do them in batches. Remove from the oven and serve, or let the pita chips cool completely and store them in an airtight container for up to 24 hours.

TUSCAN-STYLE WHITE BEAN DIP

YIELD | 4 CUPS

1	head garlic	¼	cup fresh lemon juice
1	tablespoon + ⅓ cup extra-virgin olive oil	1	teaspoon dried rosemary
2	cans (15 ounces each) white cannellini beans, drained and rinsed		Coarse salt and ground white pepper to taste

Preheat the oven to 350°F.

Slice the top from the head of the garlic, exposing the tops of the cloves. Rub the entire head with the 1 tablespoon oil, wrap in aluminum foil, place on a baking sheet, and bake until fork-tender, about 45 minutes. Remove the garlic from the foil, remove the papery skins, slit each clove with a bird's beak or small paring knife, and push the garlic into a small bowl. Mash and set aside.

In a large bowl, mash the beans with a potato masher or the back of a wooden spoon. (You can use a food processor, but do not pulse to a paste, and remove the beans to a bowl before adding the other ingredients.) Add the lemon juice, rosemary, reserved garlic, and the remaining ⅓ cup oil, and season with salt and pepper to taste. Serve immediately or refrigerate, covered, for up to 24 hours.

To serve the dish: Serve this spread at room temperature on Crostini (page 11) or slices of crusty bread.

HOT CRAB DIP

YIELD | 6 CUPS

1	pound backfin crabmeat	1	tablespoon Worcestershire sauce
12	ounces (about 1½ cups) cream cheese, softened	½	cup grated cheddar cheese
8	ounces (1 cup) sour cream	¼	cup dry sherry (optional)
½	cup mayonnaise		Salt and pepper
1	tablespoon Old Bay seasoning		Sweet paprika for garnish

Preheat the oven to 350°F.

In a large bowl, combine all the ingredients, then place in an all-temperature dish that can go from the refrigerator to the oven. Bake until the dish bubbles a bit, about 30 minutes.

Remove from the oven and let stand for at least 20 minutes. Do not serve directly from the oven, as the center will be scalding.

The dip can be made a day in advance, cooled, covered, and refrigerated until ready to use.

To serve the dish: If you've made the dip ahead of time, heat for 15 minutes at 300°F 20 minutes before serving, so it isn't too hot. Serve with spoons so people can place the dip on Crostini (page 11), Toasted Polenta Slices (page 24), or crackers.

POTLUCK NOTE | *Backfin crabmeat is good for this dish because it is a little richer in taste and a little less expensive than lump and much better than canned. It often has some bits of shell that you have to pick out and discard.*

ARTICHOKE–SPINACH DIP

YIELD | 8 CUPS

8	ounces (about 1 cup) cream cheese, at room temperature	2	boxes (10 ounces each) frozen chopped spinach, thawed and drained
3	cloves garlic, minced	2	jars (14 ounces) marinated artichoke hearts, drained and minced
1	cup light mayonnaise		
⅔	cup shredded Parmesan cheese		
⅔	cup shredded Monterey Jack cheese		

Preheat the oven to 325°F.

In a large bowl, using an electric mixer or by hand, blend the cream cheese, garlic, mayonnaise, Parmesan, and Monterey Jack. Fold in the spinach and artichokes.

Place the mixture in an ovenproof serving dish and bake until the edges are bubbling, about 45 minutes.

To serve the dish: This can be served with Crostini (page 11), Toasted Polenta Slices (page 24), or any type of cracker.

Tomato-Peach Salsa (opposite)
Crispy Pita Chips (page 14)

TOMATO–PEACH SALSA

This delicious fruity salsa is perfectly paired with Crispy Pita Chips (page 14).

YIELD | 4 CUPS

4	ripe peaches, chopped, or 8 canned peach halves	1	tablespoon fresh lime juice
8	plum tomatoes, peeled and chopped	1	tablespoon vinegar
1	sweet or red onion, chopped	1	tablespoon grated fresh ginger or 1½ teaspoons ground
1	tablespoon + 1 teaspoon packed brown sugar	2	tablespoons minced fresh cilantro
			Salt

In a large bowl, combine all the ingredients except the salt, cover, and refrigerate for at least 2 hours or up to 24 hours. Taste and season with salt if necessary.

To serve the dish: This is a great accompaniment to Dilled Shrimp (page 21), Chicken Satay Skewers (page 9), or any cheese and cold-cut plates that you may arrange.

DEVILED EGGS

12	hard-cooked eggs, chilled and peeled		Salt and pepper to taste
2	tablespoons mayonnaise	2	tablespoons minced fresh cilantro or flat-leaf parsley, for garnish
1	teaspoon mild curry powder		
2	tablespoons sweet chutney, such as Major Grey's, minced		

Halve each egg lengthwise and remove the yolks to a mixing bowl. Mash the yolks and stir in the mayonnaise, curry, and chutney. Season with salt and pepper to taste.

Gently spoon the egg-yolk mixture back into the egg whites and mound the filling with a butter knife. Place the deviled eggs in an egg holder or platter and cover.

To serve the dish: When you're ready to serve, garnish each egg with a little sprinkle of the cilantro or parsley.

POTLUCK NOTE | *To hard-cook eggs, place them in a pot with water to cover by 2 inches. Do not crowd them. Bring to a boil and cook for 1 minute. Then remove from the heat, cover the pot, and let stand for 12 minutes for one to six eggs, 20 minutes for more. Remove the eggs from the pot with a slotted spoon, place them in a bowl in the sink, and run cold water over them until the shells are cool to the touch. You can refrigerate the eggs in their shells for up to 3 days. To remove the shell, crackle it by tapping the egg gently on the edge of a bowl or cup. Roll the egg between your hands to loosen the shell. If the shell sticks, hold the egg under running water to help ease off the shell smoothly.*

DILLED SHRIMP

Shrimp

¼	cup salt + more to taste
½	cup sugar
1	bunch fresh dill or ¼ cup dried

2	pounds medium (30–40 count/pound) fresh or frozen shrimp

Marinade

½	cup canola oil
¼	cup white wine vinegar
½	cup minced fresh dill or 3 tablespoons dried

Salt and pepper to taste

Sprigs of fresh dill or parsley, for garnish

To make the shrimp: Fill a stockpot with water and add the ¼ cup salt, sugar, and dill. Bring to a boil. Drop the shrimp in and boil rapidly for 4 to 5 minutes. Turn off the heat and leave the shrimp in the pot another 5 minutes.

Drain the shrimp and run under cold water to stop the cooking. Peel and devein the shrimp, then place in a 9-by-13-inch Pyrex baking dish.

To assemble the dish: In a small bowl, combine the oil, vinegar, dill, and salt and pepper to taste, then pour the marinade over the shrimp, stirring until the shrimp are covered. Cover with plastic wrap and refrigerate for 2 to 3 hours or up to 24 hours. If you are transporting the shrimp, carry them in a thermal container with a cold pack.

To serve the dish: Arrange the dill or parsley sprigs on a serving platter. Lift the shrimp from the baking dish with a slotted spoon and load them onto the platter. This simple shrimp dish can be served with a classic cocktail sauce or Tomato-Peach Salsa (page 19).

SMOKED SALMON–POTATO CUPS

1–2	pounds fingerling potatoes (about 20), each 1–2 inches in diameter and 3 inches long	3	tablespoons minced chives + more for garnish
1	tablespoon extra-virgin olive oil	1	teaspoon drained small capers + more for garnish
	Salt	1	teaspoon prepared white horseradish, drained
12	ounces smoked salmon, minced		
⅓	cup (about 3 ounces) sour cream		

Preheat the oven to 375°F. Line a large baking sheet with foil.

Parboil the potatoes in boiling water until barely tender, about 5 minutes. Let cool slightly on a plate.

Halve each potato and use a small melon baller to scoop out an indentation, leaving at least a ¼-inch shell. Cut a thin slice from the bottom of each potato cup so it won't wobble. Discard these potato bits or place in a zip-top bag and freeze for use in soup or stock.

In a bowl, toss the potato cups with the oil and season lightly with salt.

Arrange the potato cups scooped side down on the prepared baking sheet and bake in the lower third of the oven until the undersides are golden, about 20 minutes. Let cool slightly.

Meanwhile, in a small bowl, mix the salmon, sour cream, chives, the 1 teaspoon capers, and horseradish. Mound each potato cup with salmon filling.

To serve the dish: Arrange the filled cups on a platter and garnish with chives and capers.

TOASTED POLENTA SLICES

YIELD | 24 SLICES

6 cups water	½ teaspoon salt
2 cups quick-cooking polenta	Coarse salt, for sprinkling
Olive oil for cooking	

Bring the water to a slow boil over medium-high heat. Pour the polenta and ½ teaspoon salt into the water, lower the heat to medium, and cook, stirring constantly, until the polenta is thick and smooth, 3 to 5 minutes (or cook according to package directions). Remove from the heat.

Spread two sheets of plastic wrap, each about 18 inches long, on two baking sheets and coat lightly with olive oil.

Divide the polenta evenly on the prepared baking sheets. With the aid of the plastic wrap and a spatula, roll the polenta into two logs, each about 2 inches in diameter. Let cool for 1 hour, then refrigerate, tightly wrapped, for up to 2 days.

When ready to bake, preheat the oven to 400°F. Line two baking sheets with foil and coat lightly with olive oil.

Remove the plastic from the logs and cut the polenta into ½-inch slices. Lay the slices on the prepared baking sheets, brush with olive oil, and sprinkle with coarse salt. Bake until the slices are golden and crisp at the edges, about 10 minutes. Turn the slices and bake for another 10 minutes, or until crisp on both sides. If you're not serving them right away, let the polenta slices cool, then layer with waxed paper in a flat carrier.

To serve the dish: Heat the polenta slices on a parchment-lined baking sheet in a 350°F oven for 10 minutes. These are terrific with almost anything, including Creamy Blue-Cheese Spread (page 14), Chicken Satay Skewers (page 9), and Dilled Shrimp (page 21).

SALADS

IN MANY WAYS, this is the easiest and most appreciated course. Large salads with lots of different ingredients are fun to put together, and you don't often get a chance to make them when you're feeding just a few people.

Most salads are easy to transport. Greens at risk of getting soggy when dressed too early can be carried separately from the dressing and toppings. Salads that benefit from early blending, like slaws and pasta and potato salads, can be made ahead of time, refrigerated, and then carried in an insulated container to your event.

Virtually all the salad dressings included here call for extra-virgin olive oil because it is flavorful, abundant, available at various prices, and quite healthy. That said, there are times when canola or safflower oil can be used if you strongly prefer it or find it convenient. Walnut, almond, avocado, truffle, and other oils can impart a special flavor. These are used so infrequently, though, that it is best to buy them in small amounts and refrigerate them after opening.

Balsamic vinegar seems to have become very popular, but though it is delicious it's not always necessary. Wine vinegars—red, white, and sherry—are good to have on hand, as are apple cider vinegar and plain white vinegar. When mixing salad dressing, it is always better to err on the side of less vinegar or lemon than more. You can always add more bit by bit, but you may need to add a ton of oil and other ingredients to correct an overly acidic dressing. Dip a bit of a leaf in the dressing to test the taste.

It's a good idea to have a few glass jars with tightly fitting screw tops in which to make salad dressing. They're easily transportable, and you just need to shake and pour when ready to serve. Keep in mind that salads are best dressed when they are completely dry.

SALADE NIÇOISE

YIELD | 10 SERVINGS

Vinaigrette

¼	cup white or red wine vinegar	½	teaspoon salt, or to taste
1	tablespoon minced shallots	¼	teaspoon freshly ground black pepper, or to taste
½	teaspoon Dijon mustard		
½	cup extra-virgin olive oil		

Salad

2	pounds fingerling potatoes	5	hard-cooked eggs (see page 20), peeled and quartered lengthwise
1	pound haricots verts or tiny green string beans	3	tomatoes, peeled and quartered lengthwise, or 1 pint cherry tomatoes, halved
1	head Boston or Bibb lettuce, rinsed and dried		
1	red bell pepper, julienned	1	cup Niçoise olives
1	yellow bell pepper, julienned	20	caper berries with stems or 3 tablespoons drained jarred capers
2	cans (6 ounces each) Italian tuna packed in olive oil		
1	can (2 ounces) flat anchovies, drained		

To make the vinaigrette: Whisk all the ingredients in a jar with a screw top. Cover and set aside. Shake before each use.

To make the salad: Place the potatoes in a large saucepan with cold water to cover by 1 inch. Bring to a boil and cook until fork-tender, about 15 minutes. When cool enough to handle, peel and toss with 2 tablespoons of the vinaigrette, then cover and refrigerate until chilled.

Meanwhile, steam the haricots verts, or drop them in boiling water for about 2 minutes; they will be crisp. If using green beans, increase the cooking time by 2 minutes. Drain in a colander and rinse under cold water immediately to stop the cooking.

To serve the dish: Lay out the lettuce leaves on a large platter and carefully arrange the peppers, tuna, anchovies, eggs, tomatoes, olives, and caper berries or capers on top of the lettuce. Drizzle with the vinaigrette and serve.

COBB SALAD

This salad, versions of which are still on menus everywhere, was named for Bob Cobb, the original owner of the derby-shaped Hollywood Brown Derby restaurant, where the salad was first composed in 1926.

Salad

½	head iceberg lettuce (about 4 cups)	2	whole boneless, skinless chicken breasts, boiled and diced
1	small head frisée (curly endive or chicory) (about 2½ cups)	3	hard-cooked eggs, chopped into small pieces (see page 20)
½	head romaine (about 2½ cups)	1	ripe avocado, peeled and diced just before serving
1	bunch watercress, bottom stems removed		
2	tomatoes, peeled and diced	¾	cup (6 ounces) crumbled Roquefort or blue cheese
6	strips crisp bacon, crumbled	2	tablespoons finely chopped chives

Dressing

¼	cup water	½	teaspoon sea salt
¼	cup red wine vinegar	¾	teaspoon Worcestershire sauce
1	teaspoon sugar	1	teaspoon Dijon mustard
1	teaspoon freshly squeezed lemon juice	1	clove garlic (any center green stem removed), finely minced
¾	teaspoon freshly ground black pepper	¾	cup extra-virgin olive oil

To make the salad: Cut all the iceberg lettuce, frisée, and romaine and half of the watercress into fine pieces and arrange in a large salad bowl. Arrange the tomatoes, bacon, chicken, eggs, avocado, and cheese in strips on the greens. Sprinkle the chives over the entire salad and garnish with the remaining watercress.

To make the dressing: In a medium bowl, blend together all the ingredients except the oil. Add the oil and mix well.

To serve the dish: Just before serving, drizzle the salad with the dressing.

GREEK SALAD

YIELD | 10 SERVINGS

Salad

1	large head green-leaf lettuce	1	cucumber
1	large head romaine lettuce	1	cup (8 ounces) crumbled feta cheese
1	green bell pepper		
6	plum tomatoes		

Dressing

3	tablespoons fresh lemon juice		Salt and freshly ground black pepper to taste
¾	cup Greek olive oil		
1	tablespoon minced fresh oregano leaves or ½ teaspoon dried		

Accompaniments

1	cup kalamata or other Greek olives, drained	1	cup pepperoncini, drained

To prepare the vegetables: Wash, spin, and dry the lettuce and tear into bite-size pieces. Cut the bell pepper in half lengthwise, remove the seeds and white ribs, and slice. Cut the tomatoes into six slices lengthwise. Peel the cucumber, cut it in half lengthwise, and remove the seeds with the tip of a teaspoon, then slice. Place all the vegetables in a large salad bowl.

To make the dressing: Whisk the lemon juice, oil, oregano, and salt and black pepper to taste in a screw-top jar. Cover and reserve. Shake before each use.

To serve the dish: Mix the vegetables and cheese, toss with the dressing, and top with the olives and pepperoncini.

FENNEL–ARUGULA–PARMESAN SALAD

There is a debate about using lemon or vinegar with Parmesan cheese. If the cheese is of the finest quality, it is probably better to omit the acid, as the cheese will have some bite to it.

YIELD | 10 SERVINGS

½   cup extra-virgin olive oil

2   tablespoons fresh lemon juice (optional)

½   teaspoon coarse salt

3   fennel bulbs, trimmed top and bottom, halved lengthwise, and very thinly sliced with a mandolin or chef's knife

3   bunches arugula, thick stems discarded

8   ounce wedge or block Parmesan cheese

In a shallow bowl large enough to hold the fennel, whisk together the oil, lemon juice (if using), and salt.

Rinse the fennel slices, dry thoroughly with a cloth towel, and toss in the oil mixture. Rinse, spin, and dry the arugula. With a V-shaped vegetable peeler, shave slices of the cheese onto a clean plate.

To serve the dish: On a large platter or individual plates, arrange a bed of the arugula, then layer on the fennel-and-oil mixture and top with the shaved cheese. Provide a pepper mill so people can help themselves to seasoning. Components can be carried separately and assembled at any destination. Carry the cheese in something that won't bend so that it doesn't crumble too much.

POTLUCK NOTE | *The pieces above the fennel bulb and some of the fronds can be wrapped and frozen for future use in soup or stock.*

COUNTRY SALAD WITH LARDONS

YIELD | 10 SERVINGS

½	pound slab bacon, rind removed	2	heads frisée lettuce
2	tablespoons minced shallots	1	log (8 ounces) room-temperature chèvre, crumbled
⅓	cup balsamic vinegar	2	cups croutons
½	cup extra-virgin olive oil		
	Salt and pepper		

Cut ½-inch cubes from the bacon and brown in a heavy skillet over medium-high heat for 10 minutes. Remove the lardons to paper towels with a slotted spoon.

Pour out the drippings and return ⅓ cup to the skillet. Lower the heat to medium, add the shallots and vinegar, and cook, stirring constantly, about 5 minutes. If you are serving the salad immediately, turn off the heat and stir in the oil. Lightly salt and pepper to taste.

To hold everything for a few hours, reserve the lardons in one container and the shallot-vinegar mixture in another. When ready to serve, heat the mixture in a small saucepan over low heat. When it is warm, stir in the lardons and remove from the heat.

Tear the frisée into bite-size pieces, wash, spin, and dry. If not serving immediately, refrigerate in a cloth salad bag or loosely wrapped in paper towels in a plastic bag.

To serve the dish: Place the lettuce in a large salad bowl, top with the chèvre, add the lardons and dressing, toss the salad, and top with the croutons.

POTLUCK NOTE | *Stale challah or brioche makes very good croutons. Remove the crust and cut the bread into ½-inch cubes. Toast on a baking sheet for 10 minutes in a 375°F oven. Use immediately, or let cool and store in an airtight container for 2 or 3 days.*

SPINACH–STRAWBERRY SALAD WITH POPPY SEED DRESSING

YIELD | 10 SERVINGS

Dressing

½	cup extra-virgin olive oil	1	tablespoon + 1 teaspoon poppy seeds
¼	cup balsamic vinegar		Salt and pepper
2	tablespoons honey		
2	teaspoons coarse mustard		

Salad

2	pints (4 cups) ripe strawberries	1½	pounds prewashed baby spinach

To make the dressing: In a bowl, whisk together the oil, vinegar, honey, mustard, poppy seeds, and salt and pepper to taste. Transfer to a screw-top jar. Refrigerate for up to 24 hours. Before serving, let the dressing return to room temperature, then shake well.

To make the salad: Rinse the strawberries, remove the hulls, and cut the berries in sixths (or quarters if they aren't very large) from top to bottom. Place in a covered container and refrigerate for up to 24 hours.

To serve the dish: Place the spinach and strawberries in a salad bowl and toss with the dressing.

POTLUCK NOTE | *The best way to rinse all berries without bruising them is to fill a bowl with water, add the berries, and let sit for a few minutes. Gently lift the berries out onto paper towels and discard the gritty water.*

BASIC MIXED SALAD

YIELD | 10 SERVINGS

1	head red-leaf lettuce	½	teaspoon sea salt
1	head green-leaf lettuce		Up to ½ cup extra-virgin olive oil
1	head radicchio	3	tablespoons wine vinegar
1	bunch watercress		Freshly ground pepper
1	red onion, thinly sliced		
1	cucumber, peeled, seeded, quartered lengthwise, and thinly sliced		

Separate the leaves of all the greens, rinse, and dry. If not using right away, store in a cloth bag in the refrigerator.

To serve the dish: When ready to serve, toss the greens, onion, and cucumber in a large salad bowl and sprinkle with the salt. Add the oil and toss to coat thoroughly. Add the vinegar and toss again. Grind a few turns of a pepper mill over the salad and serve immediately.

POTLUCK NOTE | *The proportion of dressing to salad is more or less ¾ cup of dressing to 1 pound of salad. Depending on how many other dishes are being served, this amount of salad will serve 10 and can easily stretch to accommodate a few more.*

QUICK CROUTONS

YIELD | 5 TO 6 CUPS

8	slices loaf bread		2	teaspoons dried thyme
⅓	cup canola or safflower oil + more if needed			Salt and pepper
1	clove garlic, crushed			

Preheat the oven to 300°F.

Trim the crust from the bread and cut the bread into ½-inch cubes.

Pour the oil to a depth of about ¼ inch in a heavy 10- or 12-inch skillet and heat over medium-high heat. Place the garlic in the skillet, add one layer of bread cubes, and lower the heat. Cook, turning with a spatula, until browned, 2 to 3 minutes. (Don't worry if the cubes are not browned on all sides.) Remove to a paper towel, sprinkle with the thyme, and season with salt and pepper to taste. Repeat until all the bread cubes are browned.

Place on a baking sheet and bake for 10 minutes.

If you're not using the croutons right away, let them cool completely before storing in an airtight container. You can keep these for 2 days, but 1 is better.

RED-SKINNED POTATO SALAD

YIELD | 12 SERVINGS

Salad

4	pounds red-skinned potatoes, scrubbed		⅓	cup bread-and-butter pickles, chopped
4	hard-cooked eggs, peeled and chopped		2	tablespoons capers, drained and rinsed (optional)
1	medium/large red onion, chopped		⅓	cup minced fresh flat-leaf parsley, for garnish
1	bunch scallions, chopped			
3	ribs celery, strings, leaves and fibers removed, chopped			

Dressing

1	cup mayonnaise		2	tablespoons sugar
¼	cup olive oil			Salt and pepper
2	tablespoons white vinegar			

To make the salad: Place the potatoes in a large pot and cover with cold water. Bring to a boil over high heat, then lower the heat to medium-low and boil until the potatoes are fully cooked but still firm, about 20 minutes. Test the potatoes occasionally with a fork so you can get them out of the water before they are too soft for the salad. Drain and rinse in cold water or an ice bath until cool enough to handle.

Slice the potatoes and place in a large bowl. Gently stir in the eggs, onion, scallions, celery, pickles, and capers.

To make the dressing: In a small bowl, mix the mayonnaise, oil, vinegar, and sugar. Stir well; then, with a rubber spatula, gently stir into the potato mixture. Season with salt and pepper to taste. Cover with a lid or plastic wrap and refrigerate until ready to use, up to 24 hours.

To serve the dish: Top with the parsley and serve chilled.

POTLUCK NOTE | *See page 20 for how to hard-cook eggs.*

COLESLAW WITH RAISINS AND CARAWAY SEEDS

YIELD | 8 CUPS (10 TO 12 SERVINGS)

¾	cup raisins	1	teaspoon ground cumin
1	cup orange juice or water	1	teaspoon caraway seeds
1	head firm, fresh green cabbage	¼	cup cider vinegar
2	medium/large carrots	¼	cup olive oil
½	cup finely diced green or red bell pepper	2	tablespoons sugar
1	teaspoon salt	¼	cup water
1	cup mayonnaise		

Soak the raisins in the orange juice or water for at least 1 hour. Drain and discard the liquid.

Remove and discard the outer leaves of the cabbage. Cut the cabbage into quarters and remove the hard core. Shred the cabbage either by hand or on the coarse shredding disk in a food processor. Shred the carrots the same way.

In a large bowl, mix the cabbage, carrots, raisins, and bell pepper. Sprinkle with the salt.

In a medium bowl, mix the remaining ingredients. Pour over the slaw and incorporate thoroughly. Refrigerate, covered, and mix again in 30 minutes. Cover and keep refrigerated until ready to serve, up to 24 hours.

To serve the dish: Place the slaw in a large bowl and serve with a slotted spoon to prevent excess liquid on people's plates.

COLD SESAME NOODLES

These ingredients are usually available in the Asian food section of large supermarkets or Asian speciality stores.

YIELD | 10 SERVINGS

3	tablespoons Chinese sesame paste
2	tablespoons oil from sesame paste
⅓	cup light soy sauce or tamari
¼	cup honey
4	tablespoons sesame oil
1	teaspoon hot chili oil, or to taste
½	cup boiling water
1	pound narrow Asian buckwheat noodles
6	ounces plain or flavored extra-firm tofu, diced
¼	cup light sesame seeds
¼	cup minced fresh cilantro

In a heatproof bowl, mix the sesame paste and its oil with the soy sauce or tamari, honey, sesame oil, and chili oil. Stir in the boiling water and mix until smooth.

Boil the noodles according to the package directions, drain, and place in a large serving bowl. Pour the sesame dressing over all and toss until the noodles are coated. Cover and refrigerate for up to 12 hours.

To serve the dish: When ready to serve, mix in the tofu, sesame seeds, and cilantro. Serve cold but with the chill off.

MEDITERRANEAN PASTA SALAD

YIELD | 10 SERVINGS

Pasta

1	pound farfalle or rigatoni		8	ounces smoked mozzarella cheese, diced
¼	cup olive oil		¼	pound pitted black olives, sliced
	Pinch of salt		1	red onion, diced
12	ounces frozen or drained marinated artichoke hearts		½	cup minced fresh flat-leaf parsley
2	ounces sun-dried tomatoes		1	tablespoon minced fresh basil (optional)
12	ounces (about 1½ cups) ricotta cheese			

Dressing

½	cup + 1 tablespoon extra-virgin olive oil		1	tablespoon sugar
3	tablespoons balsamic vinegar			Salt and pepper

To make the pasta: Cook the pasta in a large pot of boiling water according to the package directions, or until al dente. Drain, run under cold water, and pat dry with paper towels. Place in a bowl large enough to hold all the ingredients and toss with the oil and salt.

In a medium saucepan, bring the artichoke hearts (cut in quarters top to bottom if not already quartered) to a boil, then lower the heat and simmer for 3 minutes. Drain and add to the pasta.

Place the tomatoes in a heatproof bowl and cover with boiling water. Let stand for 5 minutes, then drain. Mince and stir into the pasta, then stir in the ricotta, mozzarella, olives, onion, parsley, and basil, if desired.

To make the dressing: In a small bowl, whisk the oil, vinegar, and sugar. Pour the dressing over the salad and toss, then season with salt and pepper to taste. Cover and chill for 1 to 2 hours and serve cold.

To serve the dish: If you are carrying this to another destination, transport the completed salad, covered, in a thermal container with a cold pack.

COUSCOUS SALAD

YIELD | 6 CUPS

3	cups vegetable or chicken broth	¾	cup shredded fresh mint leaves
1	teaspoon ground cumin	5	scallions, finely chopped
1	teaspoon ground cinnamon	½	cup coarsely chopped pistachios
2	cups instant couscous	½	cup slivered almonds, toasted
1	can (15 ounces) chickpeas, rinsed and drained	1	cup dates, pitted and chopped
½–¾	cup extra-virgin olive oil, as needed		Salt and pepper
	Juice and grated zest of 1 lemon (see page 262)		

In a medium pot, heat the broth with the cumin and cinnamon over medium heat until simmering, about 5 minutes. Stir in the couscous until thoroughly moistened. Remove from the heat and transfer to a bowl large enough to hold all the ingredients.

Toss the couscous with the chickpeas and ½ cup of the oil. Let cool, then add the lemon juice and zest and the mint. Mix in the scallions, pistachios, almonds, and dates. Season with salt and pepper to taste. Add up to ¼ cup additional oil, if needed.

To serve the dish: This dish is best served within 2 hours or so, at room temperature.

MIXED BEAN SALAD

This is a year-round favorite. You can combine any variety of beans and use your own dressing.

YIELD | 10 SERVINGS

Salad

¾	cup cooked orange lentils	2	large tomatoes, peeled, seeded, and diced (omit if out of season)
1⅓	cups cooked black beans or 1 can (15 ounces), rinsed and drained	1	red onion, diced
1⅓	cups cooked white beans or 1 can (15 ounces), rinsed and drained	3	large ribs celery, strings removed, diced
1⅓	cups cooked chickpeas or 1 can (15 ounces), rinsed and drained	2	tablespoons minced fresh basil or up to 1 teaspoon dried
5	walnut-size red radishes, halved and sliced lengthwise	¼	cup minced fresh flat-leaf parsley

Vinaigrette

⅓	cup extra-virgin olive oil	¼	teaspoon crushed red pepper flakes
1–2	cloves garlic, minced		Sea salt and freshly ground black pepper to taste
2	tablespoons fresh lemon juice		
3	tablespoons red wine vinegar		
2	teaspoons Dijon mustard		

To make the salad: In a bowl large enough to hold all the ingredients, mix the lentils, black beans, white beans, and chickpeas. Add the radishes, tomatoes, onion, celery, basil, and parsley and stir to combine.

To make the vinaigrette: In a tightly covered jar, mix the oil, garlic, lemon juice, vinegar, mustard, red pepper flakes, and salt and pepper to taste. Shake well. Pour over the bean mixture and stir to combine. Cover and refrigerate for up to 24 hours.

To serve the dish: This salad is best served at room temperature.

PASTA

PASTA IS THE UNIVERSAL comfort food. It is a blank canvas on which the world's palate is exhibited. Pasta in all its many forms is easy to cook, and most of the sauces included here can be made several days ahead. Many of the composed dishes can be assembled a day before you want to serve them. The dish can be made at home and then transported in an insulated carrier or cooked at your destination. (Pyrex and other companies make insulated meal carriers that have covered, variously sized freezer-to-oven dishes with hot or cold gel packs.) It is generally a good idea to use short pasta such as ziti or rigatoni instead of spaghetti or linguine if food is being served buffet- or family-style, because it retains an al dente quality and is easy to portion out.

Pasta will vary in size according to the manufacturer, so use these measurements as guidelines. When using shaped, small-to-medium pasta such as bow ties, elbow pasta (macaroni), farfalle, fusilli, penne, rigatoni, rotelle (wagon wheels), shells, and ziti: One-half pound will yield 4 cups of cooked pasta. Long pasta will be about the same: One-half pound of spaghetti, linguine, fettuccine, or similar pastas will also yield 4 cups cooked. For egg noodles, ½ pound will yield about 2½ cups. Depending on how it is served and what accompanies it, ½ pound of pasta will serve four to six people.

Traditionally, 1 pound of pasta is boiled in 4 quarts of water with 1 teaspoon of salt and 1 tablespoon of oil. However, both the salt and the oil can be omitted.

When boiling pasta, taste a bit to make sure that it is al dente, not raw. As a rule, fresh store-bought pasta needs to be in boiling water for 5 minutes; packaged dry pasta, 10; and whole wheat, 12 to 15. For hot dishes, drain but don't rinse the pasta unless otherwise directed, and reserve a cup of the cooking water to use if water is needed in the sauce. For cold dishes, drain, rinse, and toss with a tablespoon or so of good olive oil, then cool.

BOLOGNESE SAUCE

This thick, rich, meaty ragù alla Bolognese derives its name from the Bologna region of Italy, where variations of this sauce are served on pasta or gnocchi.

YIELD | 6 CUPS

¼	cup extra-virgin olive oil	¾	teaspoon salt
1	carrot, finely chopped	½	teaspoon freshly grated or ground nutmeg
2	large ribs celery, diced		
1	medium/large onion, diced	2	tablespoons tomato paste
2	tablespoons unsalted butter	2	cans (28 ounces each) Italian diced tomatoes, 1 drained
1	pound ground beef		Salt and freshly ground pepper
1	pound skirt steak, minced	½	cup heavy cream
1	cup dry Italian white wine		
1	cup whole milk		

Heat the oil in a Dutch oven (which will hold a uniform temperature without scorching) over medium-high heat. Add the carrot, celery, and onion. Reduce the heat to medium and cook, stirring, until the pan becomes dry, about 10 minutes. Stir in the butter. Add the ground beef and steak and cook, stirring occasionally, until the meat browns evenly, about 20 minutes.

Add the wine and cook, stirring, for 5 minutes. Gradually add the milk. Stir in the salt, nutmeg, and tomato paste, then pour in the tomatoes. Stir to scrape the bottom of the Dutch oven. Reduce the heat to medium-low and cook, uncovered, for 30 minutes, stirring occasionally. Reduce the heat to low and simmer, stirring occasionally, for 3 hours. Add salt and pepper to taste. Stir in the cream.

The sauce can be cooled, covered, and refrigerated for up to 3 days. To heat, simmer on low heat for 20 minutes, stirring frequently, before serving.

POTLUCK NOTE | *To grate nutmeg, you can use either a small grater meant for this purpose, or a Microplane. You can also use a nutmeg mill, which looks like an oversize pepper mill. You can find these items at any kitchenware store or online.*

SAUSAGE-AND-PEPPERS PASTA CASSEROLE

YIELD | 10 SERVINGS

5	tablespoons olive oil	1½	cups water
1½	pounds Italian sausage (sweet, hot, or a combination), cut into 1-inch pieces	1	teaspoon dried oregano
		1	teaspoon dried thyme
		1	teaspoon dried rosemary
2	red bell peppers, cored and sliced	½	teaspoon black pepper
2	green bell peppers, cored and sliced	1	pound penne, cooked al dente and drained
2	large onions, sliced	¼	cup shredded Parmesan cheese
1	can (28 ounces) roasted or regular diced tomatoes		
1	can (6 ounces) tomato paste		

Preheat the oven to 350°F.

Heat 3 tablespoons of the oil in a large skillet over medium heat. Cook the sausage until brown, about 10 minutes. Remove the sausage from the skillet and set aside.

Place the red and green bell peppers and onions in the skillet and sauté until the onions are transparent and golden brown, about 10 minutes. Return the reserved sausage to the skillet and add the tomatoes, tomato paste, water, oregano, thyme, rosemary, and black pepper. Mix very well. Cook and stir for 5 minutes over low heat.

In a bowl large enough to hold all the ingredients, stir the penne with the remaining 2 tablespoons olive oil. Stir in the sausage-and-peppers mixture. At this point, the mixture can be covered and refrigerated for up to 24 hours.

To serve the dish: Transfer the mixture to a casserole and bake until piping hot and the sausage is cooked through, about 45 minutes. Remove from the oven and sprinkle with the cheese.

LASAGNA WITH BÉCHAMEL SAUCE

This is another of those amazing Italian classics that seems complicated the first time you prepare it, and yet some version of this dish is the mainstay at a great many potlucks. Make it your own. Use your favorite tomato sauce instead of those suggested here. Try the "no cook" lasagna noodles available at many supermarkets, using 24 sheets from two 8-ounce packages. You might even try spinach lasagna, if your supermarket carries it.

YIELD | 10 SERVINGS

¼	cup extra-virgin olive oil or spray, for coating pan and pasta	1½	cups diced mozzarella cheese
2	packages (8 ounces each) lasagna noodles	4	cups Parmesan Béchamel Sauce (recipe follows)
4	cups Thick Tomato and Meat Sauce (see page 58) or Bolognese Sauce (see page 45)	½	cup grated Parmesan cheese, for topping
1	container (15 ounces) ricotta cheese, drained		

Preheat the oven to 375°F. Oil the bottom and sides of a 12-by-16-inch lasagna pan or 3½-inch deep roasting pan and set aside.

Cook and drain the lasagna noodles according to package directions. Brush or spray with olive oil.

Place a thin layer of tomato sauce in the pan and spread with a rubber spatula. Place a single layer of noodles over all, overlapping them slightly. Cover with a layer of tomato sauce, then dot with teaspoons of the ricotta and about one-fourth of the mozzarella. Cover with 1 cup of Béchamel Sauce. Continue layering until all the noodles are used, ending with mozzarella cheese and Béchamel.

Bake until the top is golden brown, about 20 minutes. Let the lasagna rest for 15 minutes before serving.

The dish can be assembled at home and baked at your destination.

To serve the dish: Cut the lasagna into squares in the baking dish and place the dish on a heat-proof mat or trivet. Serve with an angled spatula or two serving spoons. Put the Parmesan in a bowl alongside. Accompany with warm sliced Italian or garlic bread—or both.

POTLUCK NOTE | *Both the tomato and Béchamel sauces are best used warm to assemble the lasagna. If you are not using them immediately, they can be cooled, covered, and refrigerated. (Freeze any extra tomato sauce.) The tomato sauce can be heated over a low flame. The Béchamel scorches easily, so it is best to heat in the top of a double boiler or on a heat tamer—an inexpensive gadget that looks like a hollow disk of light metal with a lot of air holes. It keeps the cooking pot from direct contact with the heat source.*

Parmesan Béchamel Sauce

3½	cups whole or 2% milk	¼	teaspoon salt
6	tablespoons unsalted butter	½	teaspoon nutmeg
4	tablespoons instant flour	¾	cup grated Parmesan cheese

In a saucepan over medium heat, scald the milk (bring it to a very low boil; just small bubbles around the edge) and remove from the heat.

In a heavy-bottomed saucepan large enough to hold all the ingredients, melt the butter and stir in the flour until the mixture is well incorporated, just before the flour starts to color, about 2 minutes. Slowly stir in the hot milk, ½ cup at a time. Add the salt and nutmeg and stir in the cheese.

SHELLS STUFFED WITH BROCCOLI, RICOTTA, PINE NUTS, AND RAISINS

YIELD | 10 SERVINGS

Pasta

20	jumbo pasta shells
3	tablespoons extra-virgin olive oil
1	cup diced fresh mushrooms
3	cups shredded and chopped broccoli, thick woody stems removed
½	cup minced shallots
2	tablespoons pine nuts
3	tablespoons raisins
1	container (15 ounces) ricotta cheese, drained
2	cups shredded mozzarella cheese + more for garnish
⅓	cup grated Parmigiano-Reggiano cheese
2	large eggs, lightly beaten
½	teaspoon salt
¼	teaspoon pepper
¼	cup chopped fresh basil or 1 teaspoon dried

Sauce

1	can (28 ounces) crushed tomatoes
2	tablespoons extra-virgin olive oil
1	teaspoon sea salt
1	teaspoon sugar
½	teaspoon garlic powder
	Salt and pepper
⅓	cup fine, unseasoned, dry bread crumbs

Preheat the oven to 350°F.

To make the pasta: In a large pot of boiling water, cook the shells, 10 at a time if necessary, for 8 minutes, or according to package directions. Gently transfer with a slotted spoon to a bowl of cold water until you've made the filling.

In a sauté pan, heat the oil over medium heat. Add the mushrooms, broccoli, and shallots and sauté until the broccoli is crisp-tender, about 10 minutes. Stir in the pine nuts and raisins and cook for 2 minutes longer. Remove from the heat.

(continued)

In a large bowl, combine the ricotta, mozzarella, Parmigiano-Reggiano, eggs, salt, pepper, and basil, then stir in the sautéed vegetables.

Remove the cooked shells from the water with a large slotted spoon and drain. Set them on a waxed paper–lined baking sheet. Gently spoon the vegetable-cheese mixture into the shells and reserve.

To make the sauce: In a saucepan large enough to hold all the sauce ingredients, bring the tomatoes, oil, sea salt, sugar, and garlic powder to a simmer over medium heat, and cook for 15 minutes, stirring occasionally. Season with salt and pepper to taste. Stir in the bread crumbs and remove from the heat.

At this point, both the reserved stuffed shells and the sauce can be cooled, covered, and refrigerated for up to 24 hours.

To assemble the dish: Spread a thin coating of the sauce on the bottom of a 15-by-11-inch baking dish. Set the stuffed shells in the dish open side up and top with the remaining sauce. Bake for 45 minutes. You can bake the dish at home and carry it in a thermal container, or bake it at your destination.

To serve the dish: Serve right from the baking dish. Garnish with mozzarella cheese.

FRESH FETTUCCINE WITH CRIMINI MUSHROOMS

2	cups boiling water	½	cup pine nuts
3	ounces dried porcini mushrooms, washed		Salt and black pepper
		1½	pounds fresh fettuccine
4	tablespoons extra-virgin olive oil	½	pint (1 cup) heavy cream
3	tablespoons chopped shallots	¼	cup shredded fresh basil
6	cloves garlic, minced	½	cup coarsely grated Parmigiano-Reggiano cheese
½	teaspoon crushed red pepper flakes		
1	pound cremini mushrooms, sliced		

In a heatproof bowl, pour the boiling water over the porcini mushrooms and let soak for 30 minutes. Meanwhile, bring a large pot of water to a boil for the fettuccine.

In a large sauté pan, heat the oil over medium heat and add the shallots, garlic, and red pepper flakes. Sauté until the shallots and garlic are golden brown, about 3 minutes. Add the porcini and crimini mushrooms and sauté for 5 minutes, then stir in the pine nuts and cook until lightly browned, about 3 minutes. Season with salt and black pepper to taste, stir, and reduce the heat to low.

Cook the fettuccine for 6 minutes, or according to package directions. Drain but do not rinse.

Slowly stir the cream into the mushroom mixture and cook until heated through, 3 to 5 minutes.

To serve the dish: Stir the cooked pasta into the sauce and immediately pour into a warmed serving dish. Top with the basil and cheese.

POTLUCK NOTE | *If you like, you can serve this dish as a casserole. Place the finished product in a large bake-and-serve dish, cover with plastic wrap, and refrigerate for up to 24 hours. At your destination, heat covered with foil in a 325°F oven for 20 minutes. Remove the foil for the last 5 minutes.*

GREEN PASTA WITH POTATOES AND PESTO

This dish is best served when you are hosting or when you can make everything but the Pesto (which can be made ahead of time) at your destination.

YIELD | 10 SERVINGS

1	teaspoon sea salt	1½	cups Pesto (recipe follows)
4	medium/large red potatoes, peeled and diced	1	cup freshly grated Parmigiano-Reggiano cheese, for serving
1½	pounds fresh or dried spinach fusilli or other short pasta		Freshly ground pepper, for serving
3	tablespoons olive oil		

Bring a large pot of water to a boil with the sea salt. Add the potatoes and cook for 5 minutes, then add the pasta and continue cooking for 5 minutes for fresh pasta, 10 minutes for dried.

Drain the potatoes and pasta, reserving ½ cup of the cooking water. Place the potatoes and pasta in a large bowl and stir with the oil and reserved cooking water. Stir in the Pesto and toss lightly.

If you prepare this dish at home, carry it in a thermal container to your destination.

To serve the dish: Serve with the cheese and freshly ground pepper.

Pesto

This recipe is best made with a mortar and pestle, but it's fine to use a blender. Just be sure to grate the cheese separately and stir it into the basil mixture by hand when it has been removed from the blender. Feel free to vary the recipe to suit your own tastes. Not to worry: Everyone in Genoa has his or her own version.

YIELD | 3 CUPS

5	cloves garlic, halved, center green cores removed	1	cup extra-virgin olive oil, preferably Italian
½	teaspoon sea salt, or to taste	½	cup finely grated pecorino cheese
3	cups shredded fresh basil leaves, center stems removed	½	cup finely grated Parmigiano-Reggiano cheese
¾	cup pine nuts		

If you are using a blender, pulse all the ingredients together except the cheeses. With a rubber spatula, remove the mixture from the blender and place in a bowl. Thoroughly mix in the cheeses.

If you are using a mortar and pestle, crush the garlic and salt until a paste forms. Gradually add the basil and keep grinding until all the basil is incorporated. Add the pine nuts and continue grinding. When a coarse paste forms, add the cheeses and gently incorporate. Add the oil and quickly blend all together with a wooden spoon.

Divide the Pesto into two 1½-cup portions. Use one portion for the Green Pasta with Potatoes, and reserve the rest for another use.

Use immediately or refrigerate, covered, for 3 days.

POTLUCK NOTE | *Pesto can be made without the cheese when basil is in season and frozen in airtight plastic containers until needed. The cheese will keep in the refrigerator for several weeks if well-wrapped. Thaw the pesto and stir in the cheese as needed.*

THE BEST SPAGHETTI AND MEATBALLS

Spaghetti is the traditional pasta for this dish, but there are many delicious alternatives if you think it will be a little hard to handle for your event. Two good pasta options for this dish are bucatini, long tubes of pasta that can be broken into 3- or 4-inch pieces, and rigatoni.

YIELD | 24 SMALL MEATBALLS

2	pounds ground beef	2	tablespoons minced fresh flat-leaf parsley
2	large eggs		Salt and freshly ground pepper
1	tablespoon olive oil + more for cooking meatballs	1½–2	pounds spaghetti
2	cloves garlic, crushed		Thick Tomato and Meat Sauce (see page 58), for serving
⅓	cup fine, dry bread crumbs		
2	tablespoons grated Parmesan cheese	1½	cups freshly grated Parmigiano-Reggiano cheese, for serving

To make the meatballs: In a large bowl, with a light touch, mix the beef, eggs, the 1 tablespoon oil, garlic, bread crumbs, Parmesan, and parsley and season with salt and pepper to taste. Do not overmix, or the meatballs will be tough. Form into twenty-four 1- to 1½-inch meatballs.

In a large heavy skillet, with up to ¼ inch of oil over medium-high heat, add the meatballs in a single layer and sauté, turning carefully so that they keep their shape and are evenly cooked, for 15 minutes, or until cooked through. If you do not have a large skillet, cook the meatballs in batches. Remove from the skillet with a slotted spoon and drain on paper towels.

If you are not using the meatballs immediately, let cool, then refrigerate in a covered container for up to 3 days. They can also be frozen for up to 1 month. Thaw in the refrigerator before using.

To make the pasta: Bring a large pot of water to a boil and cook the pasta according to package directions. This is not a dish that requires the pasta to be al dente. However, it is best if cooked just before serving.

To serve the dish: Drain the pasta and place in a warm, deep platter; toss with Thick Tomato and Meat Sauce; and top with the meatballs. Serve with a generous bowl of Parmigiano-Reggiano. Warm Italian bread makes a good accompaniment.

POTLUCK NOTE | *Dried pasta can be boiled until al dente, drained, and tossed with a light coating of extra-virgin olive oil. Let cool and refrigerate for up to 2 days. Before serving, place in a large pot of boiling water, stir, bring the water back to a boil, remove after 1 minute, drain, and proceed with the recipe directions.*

THICK TOMATO AND MEAT SAUCE

This versatile sauce can be used for any recipe calling for a rich tomato sauce, not just spaghetti and meatballs.

YIELD | 2 QUARTS (8 ONE-CUP OR 16 HALF-CUP SERVINGS)

½	cup olive oil	5	tablespoons tomato paste
4	pork chops	1	head garlic, peeled and crushed
1	large onion, diced	2	tablespoons chopped fresh oregano or 2 teaspoons dried
3	large ribs celery, diced		
2	carrots, shredded	½	cup chopped fresh flat-leaf parsley
1	pound fresh mushrooms, sliced	1	cup dry red wine
4	pounds tomatoes, peeled, seeded and crushed, or 2 cans (28 ounces each) Italian crushed tomatoes	½	lemon, quartered and seeded
		2	tablespoons sugar

Heat ¼ cup of the oil in a large heavy saucepan over medium-high heat. Cook the pork chops until browned on both sides, about 2 minutes per side. Add the onion, celery, and carrots and cook until slightly browned, about 2 minutes. Stir in the mushrooms and add more of the remaining oil as needed. Add the remaining ingredients and simmer for 3 hours, stirring frequently. (If using canned tomatoes, drain 1 can and use the liquid from the other.)

After 2½ hours, remove the pork chops. Remove the pork from the bones, shred it, and return the meat to the sauce. Remove the lemon pieces and discard. If the sauce is too thick, add some wine or some water splashed with balsamic vinegar.

The sauce can be cooled and refrigerated for 3 days if you are not using it immediately. To freeze it, ladle the cooled sauce into two tightly sealed 1-quart containers and label them with the contents and the date. The sauce can be kept frozen for 1 month.

If you make this sauce ahead of time and refrigerate it, simmer it on low heat for 15 minutes, stirring frequently, before serving.

MINESTRONE WITH PESTO

There are many versions of this delicious soup. If you don't have cannellini beans, substitute any white bean or even red ones. No turnip? Use carrots and zucchini. To make this meatless, omit the bacon and use 4 tablespoons of extra-virgin olive oil. You will soon make this recipe your own. With bread and a salad, dinner is ready.

YIELD | 4 QUARTS (16 ONE-CUP SERVINGS)

¼	pound bacon, diced	1	cup fresh peas (frozen may be substituted)
1	large onion, chopped		
3	leeks, white and light green parts only, well rinsed and chopped	1	cup cut string beans, (1-inch pieces)
1	turnip, peeled and chopped	1½	cups cooked, rinsed, and drained canned cannellini beans
3	cups shredded cabbage	1	large red potato, peeled and diced
2	teaspoons coarse salt	¼	pound tubetti pasta or small macaroni
½	teaspoon freshly ground pepper		
8	cups water		Pesto (see page 55), for topping
3	large tomatoes, diced	1	cup freshly grated or store-bought Parmesan cheese, for topping
2	cloves garlic, minced		
6	basil leaves		

In a heavy-bottomed soup pot large enough to hold all the ingredients, over medium heat, sauté the bacon, onion, leeks, turnip, and cabbage. Stir continuously until the onion is golden brown, about 7 minutes.

Stir in the salt, pepper, water, tomatoes, garlic, and basil and increase the heat to medium-high. Stir in the peas, string beans, cannellini beans, and potato. Bring to a slow boil, lower the heat, and simmer uncovered for 30 minutes. At this point the soup can be cooled, covered, and refrigerated for up to 2 days.

Before serving, bring to a low boil, add the pasta, and cook until the pasta is cooked through, about 12 minutes. As an alternative, the pasta can be cooked separately and added to the simmering soup 10 minutes before serving.

To serve the dish: Serve hot, with the Pesto and the cheese in serving bowls alongside.

PASTA SQUARES WITH ROASTED VEGETABLES

YIELD | 10 SERVINGS

½	cup extra-virgin olive oil, in various uses	2	cloves garlic, minced
2	zucchini, scraped and sliced	⅓	cup best-quality balsamic vinegar, preferably aged
1	eggplant, quartered lengthwise and sliced	1	pound lasagna noodles, broken into 4-inch pieces
1	large red onion, halved and sliced	½	cup chopped fresh flat-leaf parsley, thick stems removed
3	Belgian endives, halved lengthwise, each half cut into 3 long sections		Salt and freshly ground black pepper
1	head radicchio, halved lengthwise, each half cut into 3 long sections	⅔	cup freshly grated pecorino or Parmigiano-Reggiano cheese

Preheat the oven to 400°F. Brush two baking sheets with some of the oil.

Arrange the zucchini, eggplant, onion, endives, and radicchio on the prepared baking sheets and brush with more of the oil. Roast until lightly browned at the edges, 30 to 40 minutes. Check the vegetables from time to time and turn two or three times during cooking. As they are cooked, transfer to a large bowl.

Heat 2 tablespoons of the oil in a small saucepan over medium heat and sauté the garlic until lightly browned, about 3 minutes. Add the vinegar and continue to cook, stirring occasionally, until slightly reduced, about 10 minutes. Pour over the vegetables and stir.

In a large pot of boiling water, cook the pasta until al dente, about 10 minutes. Drain but do not rinse. Mix the pasta with the vegetables in their vinegar sauce, add the remaining olive oil and the parsley, and season with salt and pepper to taste.

You can serve the dish from the bowl or as a casserole: Place the finished dish in a 9-by-13-inch deep-sided bake-and-serve dish, cool, cover with plastic wrap, and refrigerate for up to 24 hours. Bring to room temperature, remove the plastic, and cover with foil. Heat at home in a 325°F oven for 45 minutes and transport in an insulated carrier, or heat at your destination.

To serve the dish: Serve hot, with the cheese at the table.

PASTITSIO: GREEK MACARONI AND CHEESE

At first glance, this dish may seem a little complicated—it isn't. There are three easy steps: 1. Cook the macaroni. 2. Make a meat sauce and a white sauce. 3. Layer them in a baking pan. It is a real crowd-pleaser, in part because it isn't something made every day. Use Greek ingredients if they are available because the aromas and textures of each country bring something unique. Most supermarkets have international sections, and there are a growing number of specialty food stores.

YIELD | 12 SERVINGS

Pasta

1½	pounds macaroni, such as ditali or small ziti
¼	cup + 2 tablespoons Greek (or other) extra-virgin olive oil
3	cups any combination Greek mizithra or kefalotyri cheese (Italian hard ricotta or Romano may be substituted)

2	large eggs, lightly beaten
1	cup fine bread crumbs
	Freshly ground nutmeg to taste or ½ teaspoon ground

Meat Sauce

3	tablespoons extra-virgin olive oil
1	onion, diced
1	pound lean ground lamb or beef
1	clove garlic, minced
½	cup dry red wine
1	can (16 ounces) diced tomatoes, drained

2	tablespoons tomato paste
1	teaspoon dried basil
1	teaspoon ground cinnamon
1	teaspoon salt + more to taste
¼	cup chopped fresh flat-leaf parsley

White Sauce

¼	cup instant flour
4	tablespoons (¼ cup) unsalted butter
2	cups milk

½	teaspoon ground nutmeg
	Salt and ground pepper
2	extra-large eggs, lightly beaten

Preheat the oven to 350°F.

To cook the pasta: In a large pot of boiling salted water, cook the macaroni until almost tender, 12 to 14 minutes. Drain thoroughly but do not rinse.

In a large bowl, combine the macaroni, the ¼ cup oil, 1 cup of the cheese, and eggs. Set aside.

To make the meat sauce: Heat 1 tablespoon oil in a large heavy saucepan with a lid over medium heat. Stir in the onion and cook until translucent, about 4 minutes. Stir in the ground lamb or beef and cook, breaking up the meat and stirring until lightly browned, about 5 minutes. Add the garlic and wine, then cover and simmer for 5 minutes. Stir in the tomatoes, tomato paste, basil, cinnamon, and 1 teaspoon salt, cover, and simmer for 20 minutes. Add the parsley and cook uncovered for another 20 minutes. Stir frequently to allow excess liquid to evaporate; the sauce should be thick.

To make the white sauce: In a small saucepan over medium-low heat, stir the flour and butter together, then slowly stir in the milk. Stir constantly until thick, about 5 minutes. Stir in the nutmeg and season with salt and pepper to taste. Remove from the heat and let cool, stirring occasionally. Stir in the eggs.

To assemble the dish: With the remaining 2 tablespoons oil, grease a 15-by-11-inch baking pan. Spread half of the macaroni mixture on the bottom of the pan, then sprinkle with ½ cup of the remaining cheese. Add all the meat sauce in a layer, then top with the rest of the macaroni. Sprinkle with another 1 cup of the cheese. Top with all the white sauce and spread it gently into the corners. Sprinkle the remaining 1 cup of the cheese and top with the bread crumbs, then grind nutmeg over all. Bake for 45 minutes.

This dish can be carried in a thermal container to your destination—it doesn't have to be piping hot. As an alternative, you can cook it completely, cool, cover, and refrigerate for up to 24 hours. Before serving, heat in a 325°F oven for 20 minutes.

To serve the dish: Let rest 15 minutes before serving directly from the baking pan.

CINCINNATI CHILI

Cincinnati Chili is the creation of chef Tom Kiradjieff, who opened the Empress, a Greek restaurant in Cincinnati, in 1922. His ever-popular dish can still be ordered one of several ways: two-way, which is chili over spaghetti; three-way, which adds shredded cheddar cheese; four-way, which brings chopped onions; and five-way, with heated kidney beans on top, not mixed in.

YIELD | 10 SERVINGS

2	tablespoons olive oil	2	ounces unsweetened or dark chocolate
¼	pound bacon, diced	¾	teaspoon salt + more to taste
1	large onion, diced	4	cups tomato sauce
2	cloves garlic, smashed	¼	cup cider vinegar
2	pounds ground beef		Pepper
1	tablespoon chili powder	1½	pounds spaghetti
2	teaspoons ground cumin		Shredded sharp cheddar cheese, chopped onion, hot kidney beans, and oyster crackers, for serving
2	teaspoons paprika		
1	teaspoon ground allspice		
1	tablespoon ground cinnamon		

In a large heavy-bottomed skillet or an uncovered Dutch oven, heat the oil and bacon over medium heat until the bacon begins to crisp, about 5 minutes. Add the onion and garlic and cook until the onion is golden brown, about 5 minutes. Spread the beef in the pan and cook until it begins to brown, about 5 minutes.

Stir in the chili powder, cumin, paprika, allspice, cinnamon, chocolate, and the ¾ teaspoon salt. Blend well. Add the tomato sauce, reduce the heat, and simmer for 45 minutes, stirring occasionally. When all the liquid has been absorbed by the beef, stir in the vinegar and season to taste with salt and pepper. At this point the chili can be cooled, covered, and refrigerated for 24 hours.

In a large pot of boiling water, cook the spaghetti for 10 minutes, or according to package directions. Drain but do not rinse.

To serve the dish: Transfer the hot spaghetti to a large, deep platter and pour the chili over it, but do not mix. Accompany with bowls of cheese, onion, beans, and oyster crackers.

GRAINS AND BEANS

GRAINS AND LEGUMES, the oldest of foods, have sustained entire civilizations, particularly when combined with the spices and herbs of the region in which they were and continue to be cultivated. It is said that Esau relinquished his birthright for lentil porridge, and when the Dead Sea scrolls were discovered at the ancient settlement at Qumran, lentils were found among shards of pottery bowls. Today, as we have become aware that the carbohydrates we eat should be as wholesome as possible, people are turning to this food group for tasty, healthful dishes for elemental feasts.

Grains are edible seeds from plants in the grass family—among them, wheat, corn, barley, rice, millet, and wild rice (which is not actually rice). Grains, especially whole grains, are excellent sources of carbohydrates (energy), dietary fiber, essential fatty acids, and other important nutrients. Legumes, plants that have pods with tidy rows of seeds inside, are their protein-filled counterparts. They include beans, peas, lentils, and peanuts. In the midst of our nation's plenty, we are privileged to have in our markets grains and legumes in the most convenient forms—in hundreds of strains, shapes, and colors. But it is when grains and legumes are eaten together in certain combinations that they form a complete protein and pack their most powerful nutritional punch.

Grains and legumes are universally eaten whole, crushed, or ground; raw, roasted, or boiled; alone or with whatever is available. These very versatile staples can form the main course of a meal or add texture, color, and flavor to other courses. They are delicious at any temperature and adaptable to many methods of cooking and styles of serving.

Conveniently, most cooked grains can be cooled, covered, and refrigerated for a few days. Many beans can be found not only dried but also canned and partially prepared. Feel free to substitute one form for another, but look carefully at the can and be sure to get those without additives.

POLENTA–FOUR CHEESE CASSEROLE

YIELD | 10 SERVINGS

8	cups water	2	cups (8 ounces) Gorgonzola cheese, crumbled
2	teaspoons salt		
1	pound coarsely ground cornmeal	¾	cup grated Parmigiano-Reggiano cheese
2	cups shredded mozzarella cheese		
1	cup shredded fontina cheese		

Preheat the oven to 400°F. Butter a 16-by-12-inch baking dish. If you are making this in two stages, be sure to use a baking dish that can go from refrigerator to oven.

Bring the water to a boil in a wide, heavy-bottomed pot and add the salt. (At the same time, set a kettle or pot of water to boil in case you need a little extra boiling water toward the end of cooking the cornmeal.) When it is at a steady gentle boil, add the cornmeal in a very slow stream. You don't want the water to stop boiling. Stir the cornmeal constantly with a wooden spoon to keep lumps from forming. Continue stirring constantly, about 30 minutes. The longer you stir, the better the polenta will be.

The finished polenta should have the consistency of firm mashed potatoes. If it seems too thick, add a little more boiling water, being careful never to add more than about ¼ cup water at a time. The polenta is done when it peels easily off the sides of the pot. (At this point you have a delicious side dish. Add some butter and grated Parmigiano-Reggiano, and you can serve it as it comes out of the pot!)

Pour the polenta into the prepared baking dish and smooth the top with a moistened spatula. Let cool until firm. The polenta can be covered and refrigerated for up to 2 days.

To serve the dish: Before serving, mix the four cheeses together in a large bowl and spread over the polenta in the baking dish. Bake until the cheese is melted and bubbles slightly, about 10 minutes. Serve hot.

POSOLE AND CHICKEN CASSEROLE

This Mexican dish is traditionally made with boneless pork cubes, which may be substituted for the chicken thighs. Posole is a specific kind of dried corn; if you can't find it, don't substitute canned hominy for this dish.

YIELD | 10 TO 12 SERVINGS

2	cups blue or yellow dried posole, picked over		1	teaspoon ground cinnamon
1	tablespoon coarse salt + more to taste		½	can (8 ounces) crushed tomatoes
½	cup extra-virgin olive oil		1	can (7 ounces) diced green chilies, drained
2	medium/large red onions, diced		2	cups beer
1	head garlic, minced			Freshly ground pepper
3½	pounds boneless chicken thighs, cubed		½	cup minced fresh cilantro, for serving
4	ancho chilies, stemmed and seeded		2	firm ripe avocados, diced, for serving
2	teaspoons dried Mexican or any oregano		16	ounces (2 cups) sour cream, for serving
1	teaspoon ground cumin		2	limes, cut in wedges, for serving

Put the posole in a large container and add cold water to cover by 3 inches. Let soak for 8 hours or overnight.

Drain the posole, transfer it to a pot, and add fresh water to cover by 4 or 5 inches and the 1 tablespoon coarse salt. Cover the pot and bring to a boil, then reduce the heat and simmer, covered, for 2 hours. Check every 30 minutes, adding water if needed, until the kernels have softened and begin to burst. Drain the posole and rinse well.

Heat the oil in a heavy 6-quart pot over medium heat. Add the onions and sauté until golden, 3 to 4 minutes. Add the garlic, chicken, ancho chilies, oregano, cumin, and cinnamon. Stir in the tomatoes, green chilies, and beer. Bring to a boil, stir in the cooked posole, then reduce the heat and simmer for 1 hour. Season with salt and pepper to taste.

To serve the dish: Serve from the pot or a warm platter and accompany with small bowls of the cilantro, avocado, sour cream, and lime wedges.

RICE, LENTIL, AND CHICKPEA CASSEROLE

YIELD | 10 SERVINGS

3	tablespoons extra-virgin olive oil
2	onions, sliced
2	teaspoons grated fresh ginger
2	cups cooked rice
1	cup cooked lentils
1	can (15 ounces) chickpeas, rinsed and drained
1	teaspoon ground cinnamon
½	teaspoon ground nutmeg
1	teaspoon ground cardamom
1	teaspoon crushed red pepper flakes, or to taste (optional)
1	can (28 ounces) diced tomatoes
½	cup minced fresh cilantro, for garnish
½	cup minced fresh flat-leaf parsley, for garnish

Heat the oil in a large heavy-bottomed saucepan over medium heat. Add the onions and sauté until well browned, about 5 minutes. Remove with a slotted spoon and set aside. Stir in the ginger and rice, stirring to separate the grains, and cook until lightly browned, about 5 minutes. Stir in the lentils and chickpeas, add the spices and reserved onions, and stir. Mix in the tomatoes with their liquid and bring to a boil. Reduce the heat and simmer for 30 minutes, stirring occasionally.

The rice and beans can be cooled, covered, and refrigerated for up to 2 days.

To serve the dish: If you've made the dish ahead of time, heat over medium-low heat until hot, about 10 to 15 minutes. Garnish with the cilantro and parsley and serve hot.

MEDITERRANEAN STUFFED PEPPERS

YIELD | 10 SERVINGS

Peppers

10	red and/or yellow bell peppers, 3–4 inches high	¾	cup chopped pistachios
⅓	cup extra-virgin olive oil	½	cup raisins
2	sweet onions, diced	⅔	cup chopped green olives
5	cups cooked brown rice	6	plum tomatoes, chopped
1	teaspoon grated nutmeg	¼	cup fresh mint leaves, chopped
1	teaspoon ground cinnamon	¼	cup parsley, chopped
			Salt and black pepper

Sauce

2	cups tomato puree		Dash of cinnamon
	Juice of 1 lemon		Dash of nutmeg
2	tablespoons sugar		Salt and black pepper to taste

Preheat the oven to 350°F.

To make the peppers: Cut "lids" from the peppers and carefully remove the seeds and ribs. Blanch the peppers in boiling water for 3 minutes, remove with a slotted spoon, and drain upside down.

Heat the oil in sauté pan and sauté the onions until they are transparent.

In a large bowl, mix the rice with the onions. Stir in the nutmeg, cinnamon, pistachios, raisins, olives, tomatoes, mint, parsley, and salt and black pepper to taste.

To make the sauce: Mix all the ingredients in a separate bowl.

To assemble the dish: Spread a light layer of the sauce in a baking dish large enough (12 by 16 inches should do it) to hold all the peppers upright. Gently stuff the peppers with the rice mixture and place in the dish. Top each with a pepper lid. At this point, the dish and the sauce in the bowl may be covered and refrigerated for up to 24 hours.

To serve the dish: Pour the remaining sauce over the stuffed peppers and bake until the tops are lightly browned, about 45 minutes. Serve hot or at room temperature.

WHITE BEANS WITH GREMOLATA

YIELD | 10 SIDE-DISH SERVINGS

1	cup minced fresh flat-leaf parsley		¼	teaspoon freshly ground black pepper
4	cloves garlic, finely minced		5	cups cooked or canned white beans (rinsed and drained)
3–4	tablespoons extra-virgin olive oil			
	Juice of 1 lemon			
	Zest of 1 lemon (see page 262)			

To make the gremolata: In a small bowl, mix the parsley, garlic, oil, lemon juice, lemon zest, and pepper. Set the gremolata aside.

To make the beans: Heat the beans in the top of a double boiler over simmering water until hot, about 15 minutes.

To serve the dish: Transfer the beans to a warm bowl and top with the reserved gremolata.

MUSHROOM AND ASPARAGUS RISOTTO

This risotto is a little more forgiving than the classic one cooked entirely on top of the stove. Because it can be removed from the oven and finished on a flame tamer, it doesn't need constant attention. It is made with Italian arborio or carnaroli rice, which will cook up with a creamy texture.

YIELD | 10 SERVINGS

10	cups chicken or vegetable stock
3	tablespoons unsalted butter
3	tablespoons extra-virgin olive oil
5	small shallots, minced
3	cups arborio or carnaroli rice
¾	cup dry white wine
	Salt and pepper
1	pound assorted wild mushrooms, trimmed, cubed, and sautéed

20	asparagus spears, the top 4 inches cut on an angle into ½-inch slices and blanched for 2 minutes, the rest reserved for another use
2	tablespoons chopped fresh flat-leaf parsley
½	cup grated Parmigiano-Reggiano cheese

Preheat the oven to 450°F.

Heat the stock in a 3-quart stockpot over medium heat until it simmers. Keep it simmering as you make the risotto.

In a large, ovenproof, heavy-bottomed casserole with a lid, heat the butter and oil over medium heat. Stir in the shallots and cook until wilted. Lower the heat, add the rice, and stir for 1 to 2 minutes. Add the wine and cook, stirring, until it is absorbed, about 5 minutes.

Stir in the simmering stock in 1-cup increments, season with salt and pepper to taste, and mix in the mushrooms and asparagus. Remove from the heat. Cover and bake for 15 minutes.

Remove from the oven and mix in the parsley and cheese.

To serve the dish: Keep warm on the stove top over very low heat on a heat or flame tamer and serve as soon as possible. You can carry this dish in the casserole in a thermal container with a heat pack.

WILD RICE CASSEROLE

Wild rice—which is not rice at all but a cereal grass—is native to North America and grows largely in the Great Lakes region. People have been eating it since prehistoric times; in the north-central plains, the Ojibwa, Menominee, and Cree tribes introduced European fur traders to the grain. It became known as wild rice.

YIELD | 10 SIDE-DISH SERVINGS

3	tablespoons unsalted butter, sliced	6	cups cooked wild rice
3	tablespoons olive oil	1½	cups chopped pecans
3	onions, diced		Salt and pepper
10	ounces white mushrooms, sliced	½	cup minced flat-leaf parsley, for garnish

Preheat the oven to 350°F.

In a heavy skillet over medium heat, combine the butter, oil, onions, and mushrooms. Sauté until the onions are golden brown, 4 to 5 minutes.

Transfer the onion and mushroom mixture to a casserole dish with a cover and stir in the rice and pecans. Season with salt and pepper to taste. At this point, the casserole can be cooled, covered, and refrigerated for up to 24 hours. Bring to room temperature before baking. Bake, covered, in a 350°F oven for 20 to 30 minutes.

To serve the dish: Top with the parsley and serve right from the casserole.

POTLUCK NOTE | *Wild rice is easy to make as a casserole component or as a side dish on its own. Rinse the rice in a colander under running water and drain. Add 1½ cups of wild rice to 6 cups of gently boiling salted water. Return the water to a boil, stir, reduce the heat, cover, and simmer for 30 to 40 minutes, or until the rice fluffs up. This will yield about 6 cups of cooked rice.*

GREEN LENTILS WITH PANCETTA

YIELD | 10 SIDE-DISH SERVINGS

1	pound dried green lentils (about 2¼ cups)	2	cloves garlic, minced
2	tablespoons extra-virgin olive oil	6	cups chicken broth or water
5	slices pancetta or 4 slices smoked bacon, diced	½	teaspoon salt
1	medium/large onion, diced	2 or 3	sprigs fresh thyme or ½ teaspoon dried

Rinse the lentils and drain.

In a heavy-bottomed sauté pan or saucepan with a lid, heat the oil over medium heat. Sauté the pancetta or bacon until brown and beginning to crisp, 3 to 5 minutes. Remove to a paper towel with a slotted spoon.

Reduce the heat to medium-low and sauté the onion and garlic until the onion is translucent, about 5 minutes. Stir in the lentils. Add the broth, salt, and thyme and stir well. Cover, bring to a low boil, and simmer, stirring occasionally, until the lentils are tender, about 30 minutes.

Remove the cover, drain the lentils if necessary, and return them to the pan, along with the pancetta. The lentils can be cooled, covered, and refrigerated for 24 hours before serving.

To serve the dish: If you've made the lentils ahead, heat over medium-low heat, stirring frequently, until hot, about 10 minutes. Place in a serving bowl.

Aromatic Lentil Soup (opposite)
Cheddar Cheese Biscuits (page 243)

AROMATIC LENTIL SOUP

YIELD | 3 QUARTS (10 ONE-CUP SERVINGS)

¼ cup olive oil

1 teaspoon ground ginger

2 teaspoons ground cumin

¼ teaspoon ground cloves

1 teaspoon ground cinnamon

Grated zest of 1 lemon
(see page 262)

2 onions, finely chopped

2 carrots, finely diced

2 ribs celery, finely diced

3 cloves garlic, minced

2 cups brown lentils, rinsed and picked over

10 cups water

1 pound plum tomatoes, peeled and diced

Salt and pepper to taste

½ cup chopped fresh cilantro or flat-leaf parsley, for garnish

Heat the oil in a soup pot over medium heat. Stir in the ginger, cumin, cloves, cinnamon, and lemon zest and cook until aromatic, about 3 minutes. Stir in the onions, carrots, celery, and garlic and cook, stirring frequently, until the onions start to brown, about 5 minutes. Add the lentils, water, tomatoes, and salt and pepper to taste. Cook over medium heat, stirring occasionally, until the vegetables are tender, about 45 minutes. The soup is best served immediately but can be cooled, covered, and refrigerated for up to 2 days.

To serve the dish: Serve the soup hot, garnished with the cilantro. A nice accompaniment would be Cheddar Cheese Biscuits (page 243).

POTLUCK NOTE | *To peel a tomato, bring a saucepan of water to a boil. Make a small X on the end of the tomato opposite the stem. Pierce the stem end with a fork, and hold the tomato in the boiling water for 5 to 20 seconds. Peel the skin back and discard. If you need to peel a lot of tomatoes, make an X in each, remove the stem circle, and drop the tomatoes in the boiling water. Remove them with a slotted spoon after 20 seconds. Peel with a very sharply pointed paring knife.*

TABBOULEH

Bulgur is wheat that has been cracked, steamed, and dried. All it needs is boiling water to bring it to a coarse cereal consistency in a very short time. The ratio of water to bulgur is usually 3 to 1. If after about half an hour there is still water visible, simply strain the grain to remove the excess liquid.

YIELD | 10 SERVINGS

1½	cups medium or fine bulgur	3	tomatoes, finely chopped
4½	cups boiling water	1½	cups minced fresh mint leaves
1	teaspoon sea salt + more to taste	1	cup minced fresh flat-leaf parsley
½	teaspoon freshly ground pepper + more to taste	½	cup fresh lemon juice
6	scallions, finely chopped	¾	cup olive oil

Place the bulgur in a large heatproof bowl and cover with the boiling water. Let sit for 15 minutes, stirring lightly with a fork every few minutes. If you see any water, let sit for another 15 minutes, then drain any excess.

In a serving bowl, stir the bulgur with the 1 teaspoon salt, the ½ teaspoon pepper, scallions, tomatoes, mint, and parsley. Toss with ¼ cup of the lemon juice and the oil. Season with more of the remaining lemon juice and salt and pepper to taste.

Refrigerate, covered, for up to 24 hours.

To serve the dish: Serve cold or at room temperature with fresh pita bread or Crispy Pita Chips (page 14).

POULTRY

FROM HENRY IV OF FRANCE, who famously said he wanted no one in the country so poor as not to have a chicken in the pot every Sunday, to Herbert Hoover's campaign pledge of "a chicken in every pot and a car in every garage," hollow promises have ruled the political roost. What is interesting is that in the vast world of cuisine, it is chicken that has been the icon of the good life.

Long a luxury, chicken has become an international staple. Simply roasted with rosemary and garlic or tucked into a comforting pot pie, poultry is one of the easiest foods to cook. Americans have enjoyed turkey at holidays and feasts for generations, and now it is abundant enough to be eaten at any meal.

ARROZ CON POLLO
(LATIN-STYLE CHICKEN AND RICE)

Growing up in New York provided an opportunity to eat around the world without leaving town. When I attended Columbia University, there was an increasing number of home-style Puerto Rican and Latino restaurants. Each made this dish differently. A salad of mixed greens is the perfect accompaniment.

YIELD | 10 SERVINGS

3	tablespoons extra-virgin olive oil	½	teaspoon saffron or 1 teaspoon powdered turmeric
3	pounds boneless chicken breasts and thighs, cubed	3½	cups chicken stock
	Salt and pepper	2	cups corn kernels, fresh or frozen
1	onion, diced	1½	cups mild or medium salsa
4	cloves garlic, minced	½	cup minced cilantro, for garnish
2	teaspoons dried oregano	1	cup sliced pimiento-stuffed olives, for garnish
2	cups long-grain rice		

Preheat the oven to 350°F.

Heat the oil in a Dutch oven or large flame- and ovenproof covered casserole over medium-high heat. Add the chicken and sauté until browned, about 5 minutes. Season with salt and pepper to taste. Transfer to a platter.

Add the onion, garlic, and oregano to the casserole and sauté until the onion has softened, about 3 minutes. Add the rice and cook, stirring, until opaque, about 2 minutes.

Add the saffron or tumeric, stock, corn, and salsa. Bring to a boil and add the chicken, but do not stir. Cover the casserole and transfer to the oven.

Bake until the rice is tender and the chicken is cooked through, about 20 minutes.

To serve the dish: Serve Arroz con Pollo from the casserole or in a large deep platter garnished with the cilantro and olives.

CHICKEN CACCIATORE WITH SAUSAGE AND MEATBALLS

Anyone who often cooks for a lot of people over a long period of time discovers that sometimes he or she just isn't in the mood. That's the best time to make Chicken Cacciatore. You can prepare it a day ahead or at the last minute, but the real reason to make it is that once you start cooking, you are drawn into the delicious aromas and restored to the pleasures of cooking. And as a reward, everyone seems to find this dish the epitome of comfort food. It is also a good choice when you are not sure how many people will be eating because sides of spaghetti, rice, or polenta can stretch it out.

YIELD | 10 TO 20 SERVINGS

1	chicken (3½ pounds), cut into 10 pieces	2	cans (28 ounces each) peeled Italian tomatoes
1	cup fine, dry, seasoned bread crumbs	1	can (6 ounces) tomato paste
¼	cup olive oil	1½	cups dry red wine
1½	pounds Italian-style, pale green, long frying peppers (Cubanelle or standard bell peppers may be substituted), seeded and cut into strips	1	tablespoon dried oregano
		1	teaspoon dried thyme
		½	cup minced fresh flat-leaf parsley
			Salt and freshly ground black pepper
2	onions, diced	20	Meatballs (recipe follows)
6	cloves garlic, minced	2	cups shredded Parmigiano-Reggiano cheese, for serving
1	pound sweet Italian sausage, cut into 1-inch pieces		
1	pound hot Italian sausage, cut into 1-inch pieces		

Dredge the chicken in the bread crumbs and set aside.

Heat the oil over medium heat in a Dutch oven or other heavy pan large enough to hold all the ingredients. Sauté the peppers, onions, and garlic for 5 minutes, or until soft. Add the sweet and hot sausages and cook until brown, about 10 minutes. Add the reserved chicken and cook, stirring, until golden brown, another 10 minutes. Stir in the tomatoes, tomato paste, wine, oregano, thyme, and parsley, and season with salt and black pepper to taste.

Bring to a low boil and gently stir in the Meatballs. Lower the heat and simmer for 1½ hours, stirring occasionally. Serve immediately or cool, cover, and refrigerate for up to 2 days.

To serve the dish: Serve hot with a bowl of the cheese alongside. If you've made the dish ahead, heat over low heat, stirring occasionally, until it starts to bubble, about 20 minutes.

Meatballs

YIELD | 20 MEATBALLS

1	pound ground beef	¼	teaspoon salt
⅓	cup fine, dry, seasoned bread crumbs		Freshly ground pepper
		¼	cup olive oil
1	large egg, lightly beaten		
¼	teaspoon garlic powder		

In a medium bowl, mix the beef, bread crumbs, egg, garlic powder, salt, and pepper to taste. Form into twenty 1-inch meatballs.

Heat the oil in a large sauté pan over medium heat. Add the meatballs and cook, turning, until evenly browned, 5 to 7 minutes. They do not need to cook through because they will cook in the tomato sauce. Drain on paper towels and reserve until ready to add to the cacciatore.

COQ AU VIN (CHICKEN IN WINE)

When I suggest this dish, I think of Paul Bocuse, one of my favorite French chefs, because he is a confidence builder. He knows that home cooks can prepare delicious meals if they relax a bit. His thinking would be that if the chicken and wine are of good quality and the dish is salted and peppered well, then the brandy can be omitted, and shallots or small leeks can be substituted for the boiling onions, and white mushrooms for the cremini.

YIELD | 10 SERVINGS

20	white boiling onions, peeled	½	cup brandy (optional)
2	chickens (4 pounds each), each cut into 8 to 10 pieces (or 6 pounds chicken sections, no wings)	2	tablespoons unsalted butter
		2	tablespoons olive oil
		2	pounds small cremini mushrooms
4	tablespoons instant flour	6	cups dry red wine
½	teaspoon salt		Bouquet garni (1 minced leek, 6 sprigs fresh thyme, 4 sprigs fresh parsley, and 2 bay leaves)
½	teaspoon freshly ground pepper		
4	slices bacon, cut into 1-inch pieces	2	cloves garlic, minced

Bring a pot of water to a boil and blanch the onions for 2 minutes. Drain and set aside.

Dust the chicken with the flour, salt, and pepper. It is not important for the chicken pieces to be completely coated.

In a Dutch oven or stove-top casserole, cook the bacon over medium heat until done but not crisp, about 5 minutes. Remove with a slotted spoon and set aside.

Place the chicken in the Dutch oven and cook, stirring, until slightly browned, about 5 minutes. Turn off the heat and pour the brandy, if using, over all. Using a long fireplace match, ignite the brandy and step back. The flame will go out in less than 2 minutes.

Return the heat to medium and add the butter and olive oil. Stir in the mushrooms and the reserved onions and cook for 10 minutes, stirring once or twice. Stir in the wine, bouquet garni, and garlic and bring to a low boil, stirring constantly. Add the reserved bacon, cover, lower the heat to medium-low, and simmer for 45 minutes. At this point the dish can be cooled, covered, and refrigerated for 24 hours.

To serve the dish: Remove the thyme and parsley sprigs and the bay leaves. Slowly bring the Coq au Vin back to the boiling point on the stovetop and serve hot, perhaps with Roasted Garlic Mashed Potatoes (page 155).

CHICKEN POTPIE WITH BISCUIT TOPPING

YIELD | 12 SERVINGS

1½	pounds skinless, boneless chicken breasts and thighs, cut into bite-size chunks
2	cups chicken stock
1	cup heavy cream
2	leeks (white and light green parts), rinsed well and cut into ½-inch slices
4	cloves garlic, minced
1	pound new potatoes, cleaned and cut into bite-size chunks
1	pound small white or cremini mushrooms, cleaned and halved
4	carrots, scraped and cut into ½-inch slices
3	tablespoons unsalted butter
3	tablespoons instant or all-purpose flour
¼	teaspoon ground nutmeg
¼	cup chopped fresh flat-leaf parsley
	Salt and freshly ground pepper
	Biscuit Topping (recipe follows)

Put the chicken, stock, cream, leeks, garlic, potatoes, mushrooms, and carrots in a Dutch oven or heavy-bottomed saucepan or casserole. Bring to a low boil over medium heat, stir, reduce the heat to medium-low, cover, and simmer until the chicken is tender and cooked through, 25 to 30 minutes. Pour the pan contents into a colander set over a large heatproof bowl. Reserve the liquid.

Clean and dry the pan, add the butter, and melt gently over medium heat. Stir in the flour until bubbling, but do not let the mixture brown. Add the hot poaching liquid about a third at a time, heating and stirring well between additions, until the mixture is thick and smooth, about 5 minutes. Stir in the nutmeg and parsley, then season with salt and pepper to taste. Add the chicken and vegetables and toss gently in the sauce until well coated. Cook over low heat for 10 minutes, then remove from the heat.

If you are not taking this dish anywhere right away, let the chicken-and-vegetable filling cool, transfer to a covered container, and refrigerate until needed, up to 48 hours. If you are transporting it right away, place it in a thermal container with a hot pack.

To serve the dish: At your home or theirs, preheat the oven to 375°F. Place the chicken-and-vegetable mixture in a 13-by-9-inch baking pan (or two smaller ones) and cover with the cut biscuits. Bake for 30 to 40 minutes, or until the biscuit tops are golden brown. Remove from the oven and serve warm.

Biscuit Topping

YIELD | 16 SMALL BISCUITS

2	cups self-rising flour	¾	cup milk or buttermilk
1	tablespoon sugar		
6	tablespoons cold unsalted butter, sliced		

Measure the flour and sugar into a medium bowl. With two table knives or a pastry blender, cut in the butter until the mixture resembles course oatmeal. Add ¾ cup of the milk or buttermilk and stir until the liquid is absorbed. The dough will be moist.

Place the dough on a floured work surface. Fold it over three or four times and pat it into a ½-inch-thick square or rectangle. (At this point, the dough can be refrigerated for 24 hours. Shape and bake just before serving.) Cut the dough into twelve 2-inch round or square biscuits but do not bake. Assemble and bake the potpie.

CHICKEN CURRY WITH PEACH CHUTNEY

YIELD | 12 TO 15 SERVINGS

¼	cup olive or canola oil
1	pound small (1½- to 2-inch) potatoes
1	pound small (1½- to 2-inch) turnips
1	pound small (1½- to 2-inch) onions, peeled
5	large carrots
	Salt and pepper
4	pounds skinless, boneless chicken breasts (4–5 whole breasts)
8	tablespoons (½ cup) unsalted butter, softened
1	piece (2 inches) ginger, peeled and sliced
1	clove garlic, peeled

3	tablespoons curry powder
2	cups plain yogurt
1	tablespoon ground cumin
1	tablespoon ground coriander
1	tablespoon ground cardamom
1	tablespoon ground ginger
2	cans (28 ounces each) peeled tomatoes, 1 can strained and liquid discarded
1½	cups shredded coconut, for garnish
1	cup minced fresh cilantro, for garnish
	Peach Chutney (recipe follows), for serving

Preheat the oven to 375°F. Spread the oil on a large baking sheet.

Cut the potatoes, turnips, and onions into six wedges each. Cut the carrots into 2-inch pieces, then halve each piece diagonally.

Place the vegetables on the prepared baking sheet, sprinkle lightly with salt and pepper to taste, and roast for 45 minutes. (You can roast the vegetables a day ahead and refrigerate them. You can also add the vegetables to the dish without roasting them first. Omit the oil, salt, and pepper.)

Meanwhile, halve the chicken breasts and trim. Cut each half into three strips lengthwise, then each strip into 1½-inch pieces. Place in a Dutch oven.

In a small blender, combine the butter, ginger, garlic, and curry powder and pulse until a loose paste. In a bowl, combine the yogurt, cumin, coriander, cardamom, and ground ginger. Stir the butter mixture into the yogurt mixture, then use your hands

(continued)

or a spatula to thoroughly coat the chicken in the pan with it. Add the roasted vegetables and stir thoroughly. Mix in the tomatoes and the liquid from one of the cans.

Bring the curry to a low boil over medium heat, then lower the heat, stir, cover, and simmer for 3 hours, stirring occasionally.

To serve the dish: Transfer the curry to a serving platter and garnish with the coconut and cilantro. Serve with 4 to 6 cups of Peach Chutney. (You can keep a pint in the refrigerator for 3 weeks and use it as you like, or give it as gift.) Other good accompaniments are hot white or brown rice and/or assorted Indian breads.

Peach Chutney

YIELD | 6 CUPS

2	pounds peaches, halved and pitted, or 2 cans (29-ounces) sliced peaches, drained	1–2	teaspoons crushed red pepper flakes, or to taste
1½	cups dried apricots	2	teaspoons mustard powder
1	cup raisins	1	cup granulated sugar
2	onions, diced	2	cups packed brown sugar
1	piece (2 inches) ginger, peeled and minced	4–6	cinnamon sticks (about 3 inches each)
2	lemons, seeded and diced (including peels)		Cider vinegar to cover

Cut each peach half into about eight pieces. (If using canned slices, cut each into three pieces.) Place in a large stockpot and stir in the apricots and raisins. Add the remaining ingredients and cook, stirring, over medium heat, until the mixture starts to boil. Lower the heat and simmer, stirring frequently, for 2 hours if using fresh peaches, 1½ hours if using canned.

Bring the chutney to room temperature, remove the cinnamon sticks, stir, and transfer to three 2-cup containers. If you will be using the chutney over the course of a few weeks, transfer to hinged or standard preserving jars that have been cleaned with their rubber gaskets in hot soapy water and rinsed thoroughly. Refrigerate for up to 3 weeks.

CHICKEN SALAD WITH GRAPES AND WALNUTS

This year-round favorite is simple to make and serve. It can be dressed up with garnishes such as crumbled bacon, olives, and/or croutons. You can also replace the tarragon with a tablespoon of mild curry and accompany it with Peach Chutney (opposite).

YIELD | 10 SERVINGS

6	cups diced cooked white and dark chicken	½	cup chopped walnuts
1	red onion, finely diced	¾	cup mayonnaise
1	red bell pepper, trimmed and finely diced	1	tablespoon minced fresh tarragon leaves or 1½ teaspoons dried
3	ribs celery (strings removed), finely diced	2	tablespoons extra-virgin olive oil
2	cups halved seedless grapes	1	tablespoon white wine vinegar
			Salt and black pepper

In a large bowl, combine the chicken, onion, pepper, celery, grapes, and walnuts. Stir in the mayonnaise, tarragon, oil, and vinegar, then season with salt and black pepper to taste. Cover and chill until ready to serve.

To serve the dish: Serve chilled, perhaps with a sliced tomato salad and a simple potato salad.

POTLUCK NOTE | *Buy the best chicken you can afford because the taste and texture of your dishes depend on it. There are now specific rules and regulations establishing standards for organic, free-range, and kosher chickens. These are the chickens that usually win taste tests and are worth looking for.*

OVEN-COOKED JERK CHICKEN BREASTS

YIELD | 10 TO 12 SERVINGS

1	tablespoon ground allspice	2	tablespoons minced fresh ginger
1	teaspoon ground nutmeg	4	cloves garlic, finely minced
1	teaspoon dried thyme	1 or 2	chipotle chili peppers*, soaked for 2 hours and finely minced
½	teaspoon salt	⅓	cup fresh lime juice
¾	teaspoon black pepper	⅓	cup rum
10–12	chicken breast halves, skin pierced	⅓	cup turbinado or packed brown sugar
3	tablespoons olive oil		Banana or plantain slices for garnish (optional)
2	onions, diced		

In a small bowl, mix the allspice, nutmeg, thyme, salt, and pepper. Rub on the chicken.

Place the oil, onions, ginger, garlic, and chili peppers in a small blender and pulse until the mixture resembles a thick paste with small bits in it. In a medium bowl, mix the lime juice, rum, and turbinado or brown sugar until the sugar dissolves. Stir in the oil mixture.

Place the chicken skin side up in a large baking dish and pour the oil-and-lime mixture over it. Cover and marinate in the refrigerator overnight or all day, turning once or twice.

Preheat the oven to 400°F. Remove the chicken from the marinade and roast on a broiling pan, basting with the marinade several times, until cooked through, 30 to 35 minutes. A meat thermometer inserted in one of the breasts should read 175°F. Serve immediately.

To serve the dish: You can carry the marinated chicken in a thermal container with a cold pack and cook at your destination. Garnish with banana or plantain slices, if desired, and accompany with white rice mixed with cubed oven-roasted yams.

---

* Slightly hot on the Scoville Scale (page 263). The chipotle is much hotter than the jalapeño—a definite bite but not burning for most palates.

ROASTED ROSEMARY–GARLIC CHICKEN

2	roasting chickens (5 pounds each)	2	lemons, cut in eighths, seeds removed
16	cloves garlic, peeled and sliced lengthwise		Freshly ground pepper
2	teaspoons coarse salt + more to taste	2	cups dry white wine
3	tablespoons unsalted butter	1	cup water
1	bunch fresh rosemary, a few sprigs reserved for garnish		

Preheat the oven to 400°F. Remove the giblets, neck, and visible fat from the chickens and freeze for future use or discard. Rinse the chickens under cold water and pat dry with paper towels. Starting at the neck cavity of each, loosen the skin from the breast. Using the tip of a paring knife, make small slits in skin that you can't get to with your fingers, such as the drumsticks. Slip the garlic beneath the skin of the breast and drumsticks of each bird.

Lift the wing tips of each chicken up and over the back, then tuck them under. Rub the chicken cavities with the 2 teaspoons salt and place 1 tablespoon of the butter, 2 sprigs of the rosemary, and half of the lemon in each. Rub the remaining 1 tablespoon butter over the chickens and sprinkle with some rosemary leaves. Season with a bit of salt and pepper. Pour the wine and water in the bottom of a roasting pan with a rack large enough to hold both chickens. Set the chickens on the rack and roast for 30 minutes.

Reduce the oven temperature to 350°F and roast for 1 to 1½ hours, or until a meat thermometer registers 180°F. (Insert the thermometer into the meaty part of a thigh, making sure not to touch bone.) Lift the rack from the roasting pan and remove the lemon and rosemary. Let the chickens sit for 15 minutes before carving and serving.

Meanwhile, pour the wine mixture from the bottom of the pan into a small saucepan, including any bits that have stuck to the bottom. Simmer over low heat for 15 minutes, taste for seasoning, and strain into a warm gravy boat or pitcher.

To serve the dish: Serve the chickens on a large platter and the sauce in a warm gravy pitcher. Accompany with crisp Pan-Roasted Potatoes (page 134).

MAPLE–BOURBON ROASTED CHICKEN WITH APPLE AND SWEET POTATO WEDGES

YIELD | 10 SERVINGS

4	whole boneless, skinless chicken breasts, split	4	large Golden Delicious or Granny Smith apples
4	cloves garlic, minced	3	large sweet potatoes
2	tablespoons unsalted butter, melted	¼	cup minced shallots
1	tablespoon Dijon or any mustard	¼	cup bourbon
¾	cup pure maple syrup		A few dashes of hot pepper sauce to taste
	Salt and black pepper	¾	cup heavy cream

Preheat the oven to 400°F.

Dry the chicken and trim the fat. Cut each half into three lengthwise slices and place in a shallow platter. In a small bowl, mix the garlic, butter, mustard, ¼ cup of the maple syrup, and salt and black pepper to taste and rub over the chicken. Cover the chicken and let marinate in the refrigerator while you prepare the apples and sweet potatoes. Wash and core the apples, then cut into eight wedges. Wash the sweet potatoes and cut them into pieces about the same size as the apple wedges.

In a large bowl, mix together the shallots, bourbon, hot pepper sauce, and the remaining ½ cup maple syrup. Stir in the apples and sweet potatoes. Mix well and place in a roasting pan. Roast for 35 minutes.

Remove the apples and sweet potatoes from the oven and set the marinated chicken on top. Return the pan to the oven and roast until the chicken is cooked through, another 20 minutes.

To serve the dish: If you are serving immediately, stir in the cream. Set out on a large serving platter. This dish can also be covered and placed in an insulated carrier. If you make it a day ahead, don't add the cream then. Cool the chicken, apples, and sweet potatoes in the roasting pan, cover with plastic wrap, and refrigerate for up to 24 hours. Pour the cream over all after you have heated the dish in a 350°F oven for 30 minutes or until hot.

Ramadan

CHICKEN WITH DATES AND APRICOTS

Harira is a one-dish stew traditionally served to break the fast of Ramadan. This is a variation done in two parts, so that one can please vegetarians. A good dessert might be fresh figs stuffed with goat cheese and drizzled with flavorful honey. A beverage of mint tea sweetened with honey complements these aromatic dishes.

YIELD | 10 SERVINGS

2	whole chickens (3–4 pounds each), cut into eighths
2	cloves garlic, minced
½	cup orange juice
1	teaspoon ground cumin
½	teaspoon ground cinnamon
5	tablespoons extra-virgin olive oil
1	medium–large onion, diced
1	cup dried apricots
1	cup dried pitted dates, halved lengthwise
1½	cups chicken broth
1	tablespoon minced fresh cilantro
1	tablespoon minced fresh mint
	Salt and pepper

Wash and dry the chickens, then place in a large, flat baking dish. In a medium bowl, mix the garlic, orange juice, cumin, cinnamon, and 2 tablespoons of the oil. Pour the marinade over the chicken, cover, and marinate in the refrigerator for 4 hours, stirring occasionally.

Heat the remaining 3 tablespoons oil in a large Dutch oven or other heavy pot with a lid over medium heat. Sauté the onion until golden brown, about 5 minutes. Remove with a slotted spoon and set aside.

Drain the chicken and set aside the marinade. Sauté the chicken in the Dutch oven, turning frequently, until browned, about 10 minutes. Add the apricots, dates, broth, cilantro, mint, reserved onion and marinade, and salt and pepper to taste. Bring to the boiling point, stir, cover, lower heat, and simmer gently for 30 minutes. Remove the lid and simmer until the chicken is fork-tender, about 30 minutes longer.

The dish can be cooled, covered, and refrigerated for up to 2 days.

To serve the dish: Serve hot, with Rice, Lentil, and Chickpea Casserole (page 71). If you've made the chicken ahead of time, heat over medium-low heat, stirring occasionally, until hot, about 15 minutes.

ROASTED TURKEY BREAST WITH ORANGE–CRANBERRY STUFFING

Often 4-pound turkey breasts are found frozen and on sale. They are very practical and will serve a crowd with this or your favorite stuffing.

YIELD | 10 SERVINGS

4	cups dried corn bread cubes*		Salt and pepper
½	cup minced celery	2	whole boneless turkey breasts (4 pounds each)
½	cup thinly sliced scallions		
1	cup chicken stock	2	teaspoons coarse salt
2	large eggs, lightly beaten	3	tablespoons extra-virgin olive oil
2	cans (11 ounces each) mandarin oranges, drained and coarsely chopped (liquid reserved)	½	cup orange marmalade
		2	tablespoons Dijon mustard
1½	cups dried cranberries, soaked in mandarin orange liquid for 15 minutes and drained well	2	tablespoons unsalted butter

Heat ¾- to 1-inch cubes of corn bread in a 200°F oven for 1 hour.

Preheat the oven to 350°F.

In a large bowl, mix the bread cubes, celery, and scallions with the stock and eggs. Stir in the oranges and cranberries. Season with salt and pepper to taste.

Place the turkey breasts skin side down on a cutting board. Slightly flatten with your hands, and rub each with ½ teaspoon of the coarse salt and 1 tablespoon of the oil. Spread half of the stuffing on top of each and bring the sides of the turkey around it. Wrap and tie tightly with kitchen twine. Transfer to a roasting pan, skin side up, and rub them with the remaining 1 teaspoon coarse salt and 2 tablespoons oil.

In a small saucepan over low heat, melt the marmalade, mustard, and butter and set aside.

Roast the turkey breasts, brushing with the glaze several times, until the internal temperature of a turkey breast is 170°F and the juices run clear when the meat is pierced with a fork, about 2 hours.

To serve the dish: Let the stuffed turkey breasts rest for 15 minutes, then remove the twine. Slice and serve on a warm, deep platter.

MEAT

THERE IS NOTHING random about the following selection of dishes, which have been favorites of friends and family for years. Almost all of them can be made in your kitchen and finished there or before serving at a potluck. I know many vegetarians, and most of them understand that there may be meat served at an event. They are usually the ones who bring a fabulous meatless favorite and have a wonderful time. There are some vegetarians, however, who are offended by the sight of meat on their table. In a crowd, there is not much to be done about this. If you know beforehand that the diners are primarily vegetarians—skip to another chapter.

That said, buy the best-quality meat you can; you don't want food that has been treated with hormones and other chemicals, so your preference might be organic and grain fed. One pound of boneless meat will serve three to four, as opposed to the old guideline of two servings. This isn't a diet book by any means, but it's good to remember that the most delicious pleasure of any dish is in the first five or six bites, so approach the buffet table with a light hand.

FIVE-FLAVOR BEEF

YIELD | 10 SERVINGS

4	tablespoons peanut or canola oil	3	tablespoons hoisin sauce
3	pounds boneless beef, cut for stir-fry	½	cup light soy sauce
1	package (12 ounces) firm tofu, drained and cubed	½	cup Shaoxing wine or dry sherry
		1	cup beef stock or water
2	tablespoons Chinese five-spice powder	1	tablespoon packed brown sugar
½	teaspoon black peppercorns, freshly ground	1	tablespoon sesame oil
		1	cup unsalted peanuts
1	teaspoon minced fresh ginger	6	scallions, sliced
2	star anise pods	6–8	cups hot rice, for serving

Heat the peanut or canola oil in a wok or large sauté pan over medium-high heat. Add the beef in batches and cook until browned, about 7 minutes. If the pan gets too crowded, remove the beef as it cooks and return to the pan for the final 10 minutes. Stir in the tofu and sprinkle with the five-spice powder, pepper, and ginger. Add the star anise and stir.

In a small bowl, mix the hoisin and soy sauces, wine or sherry, stock or water, sugar, and sesame oil. Stir and pour over the meat mixture. Cook for 3 minutes and stir in the peanuts and scallions. Cook and stir for about 10 minutes more, until well mixed. Remove the star anise pods.

To serve the dish: Transfer to a warm platter and serve with 6 to 8 cups of hot rice.

CHILI MOLE

This is a North American version of a dish from Puebla, Mexico, where mole poblano has been made for centuries, using shredded turkey as a base. The hundreds of varieties that have developed in the United States are often called chili Americano. Among the differences is that instead of using whole dried chili peppers and shredded poultry, we shortcut with ground chili powders and ground meat or poultry.

YIELD | 12-PLUS SERVINGS

2	tablespoons canola oil	1	teaspoon ground cinnamon
2	medium/large onions	½	cup grated dark chocolate
6	cloves garlic	¾	cup slivered almonds
1	teaspoon coriander seeds	¾	cup raisins
1	teaspoon anise seed	2–3	cups tomato juice or water, if necessary
4	pounds ground beef, or 2 pounds beef and 2 pounds pork	6	cups hot cooked rice, for serving
1	teaspoon sea salt	2½	cups hot cooked pinto beans, for serving
2	tablespoons ancho chili powder	⅓	cup chopped fresh cilantro, for garnish
3	tablespoons blended chili powder, such as New Mexico blend		Chopped olives, sour cream, and crumbled queso fresco or shredded Jack cheese, for serving (optional)
1	can (28 ounces) crushed tomatoes		
1	pound tomatillos, husked and rinsed, or diced green tomatoes		
¼	teaspoon ground cloves		

Heat the oil in a flameproof casserole or large heavy-bottomed saucepan over medium-high heat. Sauté the onions and garlic until golden brown, about 5 minutes. Stir in the coriander and anise seeds, ground meat, and salt. Blend in the chili powders, then add the tomatoes and tomatillos. Stir and bring to the boiling point. Lower the heat and add the cloves, cinnamon, chocolate, almonds, and raisins. Stir thoroughly and simmer, uncovered, for 2 hours, stirring from time to time. Add up to 3 cups liquid if the chili seems dry.

To serve the dish: If you've made the dish ahead of time, heat the chili over medium-low heat for 20 minutes, stirring frequently. Serve piping hot, accompanied by large bowls of the rice and beans and a bowl of the cilantro. Set out bowls of olives, sour cream, and cheese, if you like.

ROPAS VIEJAS (AROMATIC SHREDDED BEEF STEW)

When I lived in Santa Eulalia on Ibiza, off the coast of Spain, there were hundreds of recipes for this dish, which refers not only to the shredded meat or "old clothes" but also to the casual way in which the dish is served.

YIELD | 10 SERVINGS

1	flank steak (3 pounds), trimmed of excess fat	½	teaspoon crushed red pepper flakes, or to taste
1	large onion, coarsely chopped	1	teaspoon ground cinnamon
1	large carrot, coarsely chopped	½	teaspoon ground cloves
2	bay leaves	1	can (28 ounces) diced tomatoes, drained
½	teaspoon salt + more to taste		
¼	teaspoon freshly ground black pepper + more to taste	1	green bell pepper, skinned and julienned
3	tablespoons extra-virgin olive oil	1	yellow bell pepper, skinned and julienned
2	onions, chopped	1	red bell pepper, skinned and julienned
1	head garlic, cloves peeled and crushed	2	tablespoons capers, rinsed and drained
½	teaspoon finely chopped fresh hot chili pepper, or to taste	½	cup chopped fresh cilantro

Preheat the oven to 350°F.

Place the steak, onion, carrot, bay leaves, the ½ teaspoon salt, and the ¼ teaspoon black pepper in a 6-quart roasting pan with a cover. (Alternatively, use a baking dish covered with heavy aluminum foil.) Add just enough water to cover the steak by ½ inch.

Cover the pan and roast for 1½ hours. Remove the steak from the pan and set aside 2 cups of the strained liquid. Using two forks or your fingers, shred the beef into "rags."

Heat the oil in a large flameproof casserole over medium-high heat. Add the onions and garlic and cook until browned, about 5 minutes. Add the shredded beef and stir in the chopped chili pepper, red pepper flakes, cinnamon, and cloves. Slowly add the tomatoes and reserved roasting liquid. Lower the heat and stir in the bell peppers, capers, and cilantro. Season with salt and pepper to taste.

If not serving right away, let cool, cover, and refrigerate for up to 24 hours.

To serve the dish: If you've made the dish ahead, heat in a 300°F oven or on top of the stove, stirring frequently, until heated through, about 20 minutes. In this country, Ropas Viejas is often served with yellow rice and tortillas.

POTLUCK NOTE | *To remove the skin from a pepper, halve it lengthwise and remove the seeds. Place skin side up on a foil-lined broiler pan and broil 4 inches from the heat source for about 5 minutes, until the skin starts to blister and char. With tongs or a fork, transfer the pepper halves to a paper bag and fold the top over securely. The peppers will steam in the bag. Remove the pepper halves one by one and pull off the fine skin with a paring knife. Don't worry if some of the skin adheres, as long as most of it is removed. Use immediately or refrigerate in a closed container, covered with olive oil, for several days.*

STEAK FAJITAS WITH TOMATO–LIME SALSA

YIELD | 18 FAJITAS

⅓	cup olive oil		2	wooden skewers, soaked in water for 30 minutes
¼	cup red wine vinegar			
1	teaspoon salt + more to taste		18	flour tortillas
⅓	cup fresh lime juice			Tomato–Lime Salsa (recipe follows), for serving
2½	pounds flank steak			
2	large onions, cut into wedges		2	cups sour cream, for serving
½	teaspoon coarsely ground black pepper		18	lime wedges, for serving

In a shallow dish, stir together the oil, vinegar, the 1 teaspoon salt, and lime juice. Add the steak and onions. Cover with another plate or plastic wrap and refrigerate for 1 hour, turning once.

Coat a grill rack with cooking spray. Preheat the grill.

Remove the steak from the marinade and pat dry. Rub with the pepper and sprinkle with salt to taste.

Grill the onions on a medium-hot grill, turning occasionally, until tender, 16 to 20 minutes. Meanwhile, thread the steak onto the soaked skewers and place on the grill after the onions have cooked for about 10 minutes. Cook the steak for 6 to 10 minutes total for medium-rare. Remove the onions from the grill and set aside. Transfer the meat to a cutting board. Let stand for 5 minutes before thinly slicing across the grain.

While the steak is resting, place the tortillas directly on the grill, turning once, until puffed slightly and browned in spots, about 1 minute.

To serve the dish: Divide the steak and onions among the tortillas, then top with about 2 tablespoons each of Tomato–Lime Salsa (use a slotted spoon to avoid excess liquid) and sour cream. Wrap the tortilla around the filling, and garnish with a lime wedge.

(continued)

Tomato–Lime Salsa

YIELD | 2 CUPS

1½ cups seeded and finely chopped tomatoes, (about 3 medium)

1 large ripe avocado, peeled, pitted, and chopped

1 tablespoon seeded and chopped jalapeño chili pepper

 Zest of 1 fresh lime (see page 262)

 Juice of 1 fresh lime

3 tablespoons chopped fresh cilantro

½ teaspoon coarse salt + more if needed

 Few turns of a pepper mill

Place all the ingredients in a glass bowl and mix well. Let stand for 30 minutes. Taste and adjust salt and black pepper. Refrigerate until needed. The salsa can be made ahead, covered, and refrigerated for up to 1 day.

BARBECUED BRISKET

YIELD | 10 TO 12 SERVINGS

2	cups ketchup	½	teaspoon sea salt
½	cup packed brown sugar	½	teaspoon freshly ground black pepper
3	tablespoons soy sauce		
1	tablespoon honey	3½–4	pounds beef brisket (not corned beef)
4	cloves garlic, minced		
1	teaspoon crushed red pepper flakes, or to taste	⅓	cup extra-virgin olive oil
		2	large onions, sliced
	Dash of liquid smoke (optional)	2	cups dry red wine or stock

Preheat the oven to 450°F.

In a bowl, mix the ketchup, sugar, soy sauce, honey, garlic, red pepper flakes, liquid smoke (if using), salt, and black pepper.

Place the brisket in a roasting pan with a cover and top with the sauce. Roast uncovered for 20 minutes.

Meanwhile, heat the oil in a skillet over medium-high heat and sauté the onions until golden brown, about 5 minutes.

Add the onions and wine to the brisket and cover. Reduce the heat to 350°F and roast until tender, about 2 hours.

If you like, you can cool, cover, and refrigerate this dish overnight. When ready to go, remove any visible fat from the dish and discard. Slice the brisket. Place a layer of sauce in an oven-to-table baking dish. Place overlapping slices of brisket over the sauce and top with the remaining sauce. Cover with foil and heat in a 350°F oven until hot, 15 to 20 minutes.

To serve the dish: Slice the brisket (if it isn't already sliced), and serve on a platter with sauce from the roasting pan over all. You might accompany the meat with a big basket of warm rolls cut in half so that guests can make their own sandwiches. Serve with sides of potato salad and pickles.

OVEN-BROILED BLUE CHEESE BURGERS

3	pounds lean ground round or sirloin
1	teaspoon sea salt
2	teaspoons Worcestershire sauce
¾	pound (about 2½ cups) blue cheese, crumbled
2	tablespoons unsalted butter, at room temperature
2	tablespoons extra-virgin olive oil
	Freshly ground black pepper

10	hamburger or kaiser rolls
10	strips bacon, well cooked and crumbled
10	slices tomato
10	slices onion, raw or fried
10	leaves Boston lettuce
	Ketchup, mayonnaise, mustard, and sliced pickled jalapeño chili peppers, for serving

Preheat the broiler for 10 minutes.

In a large bowl, mix the ground beef with the salt and Worcestershire sauce and shape into 20 four-inch-diameter patties. Place 10 of the patties on a baking sheet lined with waxed paper.

In a small bowl, mix the blue cheese and butter, and divide the mixture among the 10 patties (about ¼ cup per patty). Smooth to within ¼ inch of the edge. Cover with the remaining 10 patties and pinch the edges closed. Cover with plastic wrap until ready to cook, up to 24 hours.

Brush a perforated broiler pan with the oil, arrange the burgers in a single layer, and season with black pepper to taste. Broil 5 inches from the heat source for 5 minutes, turn with a metal spatula, and broil for another 4 minutes. Remove from the broiler and turn the heat off.

While the burgers are cooking, place the rolls on a baking sheet. As soon as the burgers are out of the broiler, put the rolls in the oven (with the heat off) to warm. Remove them after 5 minutes.

To serve the dish: Set the burgers on the rolls on a large platter. Arrange the bacon, tomato, onion, and lettuce on another platter, and set out the ketchup, mayonnaise, mustard, and chili peppers in bowls. Let people choose their own toppings and dressings.

MOUSSAKA

This classic layered Greek entrée is a little bit of a fuss but one of the best potluck dishes to add to your list of dependable favorites. Rich and custardy, it is a nice change from lasagna and eggplant parmigiana, though it combines some of the qualities of each.

YIELD | 10 SERVINGS

Eggplant

2	large eggplants (about 3 pounds total)	½	cup fine, dry, unseasoned bread crumbs
	Coarse salt	¼	cup extra-virgin olive oil

Meat

3	tablespoons extra-virgin olive oil	½	teaspoon ground cinnamon
1½	onions, diced	8	plum tomatoes, chopped, or 1 can (15 ounces) diced tomatoes, drained
4	cloves garlic, minced		
2	pounds ground lamb or beef	1	can (28 ounces) diced tomatoes, drained
1	teaspoon dried oregano		
⅛	teaspoon ground allspice	2	tablespoons tomato paste
¼	teaspoon ground cloves		

Topping

4	cups yogurt	6	egg yolks
¼	teaspoon sea salt	3	tablespoons instant flour
	Pinch of ground nutmeg		

Preheat the oven to 360°F.

To make the eggplant: Cut the eggplants lengthwise into ¼-inch-thick slices and sprinkle with coarse salt. Arrange layers of eggplant in one large colander or two regular ones and cover with a heavy plate or pan. Let drain in the sink for 2 hours. This step will ensure that the eggplant has a good texture.

To make the meat: While the eggplant is draining, prepare the meat layer. Heat the oil in a heavy skillet over medium heat. Add the onions, garlic, and meat and sauté until the meat is no longer pink, about 10 minutes. Stir in the oregano, allspice, cloves, and cinnamon and cook until the meat is slightly browned, about 5 minutes. Stir in the tomatoes and tomato paste and simmer for 10 minutes more.

When the eggplant has drained, rinse it thoroughly and press down on it to remove excess water. Lay it out on paper towels to remove all moisture, and dust with the bread crumbs. Heat the oil in large clean skillet over medium-high heat and lightly sauté the eggplant in a single layer until golden brown, about 3 minutes per side. Remove to paper towels as slices cook, adding more oil and eggplant until done.

To make the topping: In a medium bowl, mix together the yogurt, salt, and nutmeg and whisk the egg yolks in, one at a time. Gradually incorporate the flour.

To assemble the dish: Brush a 10-by-13-by-3-inch baking dish with oil. Lay half of the eggplant slices in the pan, overlapping them. Cover with half of the meat sauce and smooth with a spatula. Repeat with the remaining eggplant and meat sauce. At this point, you can cover it tightly with foil and refrigerate for up to 24 hours. Refrigerate the topping separately.

Bring to room temperature and pour the custard topping over the layered mixture. Smooth with a spatula.

Bake until the top is lightly browned and the custard is set, about 1 hour. Remove the Moussaka from the oven and let rest for 10 minutes before cutting.

To serve the dish: Cut the Moussaka in squares like lasagna and serve right from the baking dish.

ROAST LEG OF LAMB WITH ROSEMARY AND JUNIPER BERRIES

Eating lamb at Easter is an ancient tradition; there was a time in early church history when it was taken to the altar and blessed before it was cooked.

YIELD | 10 SERVINGS

1	leg of lamb (8–9 pounds)	2	tablespoons chopped fresh rosemary
1	teaspoon sea salt + more to taste		
	Freshly ground pepper	2½	cups chicken or vegetable stock
2	tablespoons juniper berries, crushed with a mortar and pestle or placed in a towel and hit with a hammer	1	cup gin
		3	sprigs rosemary, for garnish
			Pan gravy
6	cloves garlic, sliced lengthwise	2½	cups prepared mint jelly, for serving
4	tablespoons olive oil		

Preheat the oven to 350°F. Have ready a roasting pan that can take the heat on the stove top.

Trim the lamb of some but not all fat and rub with the 1 teaspoon salt, pepper to taste, and 1 tablespoon of the berries. With the tip of a paring knife, make about eight tiny cuts into the lamb and insert some of the garlic slices.

Heat the oil in the roasting pan over medium-high heat, then add the lamb and sear on all sides until well browned, turning occasionally, for 10 minutes. Add the chopped rosemary, stock, gin, and the remaining garlic and 1 tablespoon berries and bring to a low boil. Remove from the heat and cover with a lid or two layers of heavy-duty foil.

Transfer to the oven and roast for 2 to 2½ hours, turning the lamb after 1 hour, or until a meat thermometer reads 160°F for medium, 170°F for well done. Remove the lamb to a serving platter, garnish with the rosemary sprigs, and let stand for 20 minutes before carving. Strain the pan juices, skim the fat, and heat for a small amount of pan gravy. Season with salt and pepper to taste.

To serve the dish: Most people like to see the whole roast on a platter, perhaps surrounded by pan-roasted or steamed new potatoes and accompanied by fresh cooked asparagus. If you prefer, the roast can be sliced and placed on a warm platter. Serve the hot gravy in a gravy boat or pitcher, accompanied by the mint jelly in a bowl.

Glazed Ham with Maple Mustard (opposite)
Sweet-and-Sour Red Cabbage (page 154)
Green Lentils with Pancetta (page 77)

GLAZED HAM WITH MAPLE MUSTARD

Ham for the holidays may go back to early Roman festivals, when pigs and boars were often roasted for celebrations. In modern history, Scandinavia and much of Western Europe celebrate Christmas from the Nativity to Twelfth Night with varieties of ham and roast pork. At Mount Vernon, George Washington savored the holidays with ham and oyster sauce as well as sweet potatoes and peanut soup. It is the maple syrup that gives this dish its American flavor.

YIELD | 10 SERVINGS

1	fully cooked, smoked, bone-in ham (about 8 pounds)	1	cup brown sugar
1⅔	cups grainy mustard	1⅔	cups pure maple syrup
			Small jar whole cloves

Preheat the oven to 325°F.

Score the ham through the rind in a traditional diamond pattern. In a medium bowl, mix together ⅔ cup of the mustard, brown sugar, and 1 cup of the syrup and coat the ham. Insert a clove into the center of each diamond. Place the ham on a rack in a roasting pan with 2 cups of water in the bottom.

Bake, basting occasionally, until a meat thermometer registers 140°F in the thickest part of the ham away from the bone, about 2 hours.

Discard the glazing mixture and let the ham rest on a platter for 30 minutes before serving.

In a small serving bowl, mix together the remaining 1 cup mustard and ⅔ cup maple syrup.

To serve the dish: The choice is yours. You can slice the ham in the kitchen and place it on a platter, or present the whole ham and carve it at the table—in which case, slice most of it and let people help themselves to seconds if it is a buffet. Serve with the maple mustard and any of your favorite mustards. Sweet-and-Sour Red Cabbage and Apples (page 154) and Green Lentils with Pancetta (page 77), each in an attractive serving bowl, are good accompaniments.

SOUTHERN HAM CASSEROLE
WITH STEWED PEACHES

YIELD | 10 SERVINGS

Roux

4	tablespoons unsalted butter	½	teaspoon garlic powder
4	tablespoons instant flour	½	teaspoon ground paprika
3	tablespoons minced onion	2	cups milk
	Pinch of cayenne pepper		

Casserole

4	cups diced cooked ham	½	cup shredded cheddar cheese
2	cups kernels, fresh or frozen corn	3	tablespoons parsley
2	cups cooked or canned lima beans, drained		Salt and white pepper
1	teaspoon Worcestershire sauce		

Topping

3	cups water	Stewed Peaches (recipe follows), for serving
1	cup medium cornmeal	
1	cup grated cheddar cheese	

Preheat the oven to 350°F. Butter a 13-by-9-inch baking dish.

To make the roux: Melt the butter in a small saucepan over medium-low heat, then stir in the flour until golden brown, about 4 minutes. Add the onion, cayenne, garlic powder, cinnamon, and paprika and stir until blended. Slowly stir in the stock or water and cook, stirring, until thickened to the consistency of heavy cream, about 3 to 5 minutes. Set aside.

To make the casserole: In a large bowl, mix the ham, corn, beans, Worcestershire sauce, cheese, and parsley. Season with salt and pepper to taste. Add the reserved roux and stir well.

(continued)

To make the topping: Heat the water in a medium saucepan over medium-high heat until boiling. Pour in the cornmeal in a thin stream and simmer over medium-low heat until thickened, about 15 to 20 minutes (or follow package directions). Stir in ½ cup of the cheese.

To assemble the dish: Pour the ham-and-roux mixture into the prepared baking dish and level with a rubber spatula. Ladle the topping over all, spreading from end to end with the spatula. Top with the remaining ½ cup cheese. At this point, the dish can be covered and taken to your destination. Bake, uncovered, until lightly browned, 15 to 20 minutes.

To serve the dish: Serve hot or at room temperature directly from the baking dish with Stewed Peaches alongside. If you're not going far, you can bake it and take it.

Stewed Peaches

YIELD | 10 SERVINGS

6	cups sliced fresh or frozen and thawed peaches (not canned)	4	thin slices of lemon, with peel, halved
1	cup packed brown or white sugar	½	teaspoon ground cinnamon
½	cup water	¼	cup bourbon (optional)

Place all of the ingredients in a saucepan. Bring to the boiling point over medium heat, stirring constantly. Reduce the heat and simmer for 15 minutes. Peaches may be cooled, covered, and refrigerated for 24 hours and heated at your destination, or served at room temperature.

PORK WITH PRUNES AND APPLES

YIELD | 10 SERVINGS

1	rolled boneless pork loin (5 pounds)	15	pitted prunes, halved, any pit parts removed
	Salt and pepper	¾	cup apple jelly
2	cups dry white wine	1	teaspoon dried thyme
3	Golden Delicious apples, sliced into 1-inch wedges	1	bunch watercress sprigs, rinsed and drained, for garnish

Preheat the oven to 350°F.

Rub the pork loin with salt and pepper and place it in a baking dish with a cover. Add the wine and surround the meat with the apples and prunes.

Cover and roast, stirring the fruit once or twice, until a meat thermometer reads 170°F, about 1½ hours. Do not turn off the oven. Uncover the baking dish and leave the pork in the hot oven.

In a small saucepan, heat the apple jelly with the thyme over low heat until melted, about 3 minutes. Pour over the pork and fruit and roast, uncovered, for another 15 minutes. Let stand for 10 minutes before slicing.

If you are transporting this dish, carry the unsliced roast and fruit in a covered thermal container with a hot pack. At your destination, heat the apple jelly and thyme and slice the pork.

To serve the dish: Arrange the pork slices and fruit on a warm platter and pour the pan juices over all. Drizzle the apple jelly–thyme glaze over all. Garnish with the watercress and serve.

PORK CROWN ROAST WITH APPLE STUFFING AND MUSTARD SAUCE

A pork crown roast is made from a 10- to 12-rib bone-in pork loin that has been tied in a circle, ribs up, to hold the stuffing. You can substitute your favorite stuffing for the one presented here.

YIELD | 10 SERVINGS

5 teaspoons herbes de Provence	1 loin crown roast (about 6 pounds)
1 tablespoon extra-virgin olive oil	Apple Stuffing (recipe follows)
1 teaspoon sea salt	Mustard Sauce (recipe follows), for serving
1 teaspoon freshly ground pepper	

Preheat the oven to 450°F.

In a small bowl, combine the herbes de Provence, oil, salt, and pepper. Rub the mixture evenly over the roast, wrap the exposed rib bones individually with small pieces of foil, and set the roast upright in a baking pan.

Fill the crown of the roast with the Apple Stuffing, mounding it in the center. Do not pack too tightly; any left over can be baked for 30 minutes in ramekins. Cover the stuffing with a piece of foil to prevent it from drying out.

Roast for 30 minutes, reduce the heat to 325°F, and roast until the meat registers 170°F on a meat thermometer, about 2 hours. About 30 to 45 minutes before the end of the roasting time, uncover the stuffing so that it can brown and crisp.

Gently remove the roast to a serving platter and let rest for 10 minutes before serving. Strain the drippings and reserve ½ to ¾ cup for the Mustard Sauce.

To serve the dish: Remove the foil from the rib bones. If you want to be festive, cover the rib tips with paper frills. Carve the roast, using the ribs as a guide, and serve with spoonfuls of Apple Stuffing and Mustard Sauce.

(continued)

Apple Stuffing

3	tablespoons unsalted butter	4	teaspoons sugar
2	tablespoons extra-virgin olive oil	1	teaspoon grated lemon zest (see page 262)
1	onion, diced		
2	ribs celery, finely diced	1	cup apple cider or juice + ½ cup more, if necessary
¾	cup chopped pecans		
2	slightly tart apples, such as Granny Smith, cored and diced	2	tablespoons minced fresh flat-leaf parsley
4	cups stale bread cubes	1	teaspoon crumbled dried sage
1	cup cranberries		Salt and pepper

In a sauté pan, heat the butter and oil over medium heat. Add the onion and celery and sauté until golden brown, about 3 minutes. Add the pecans and roast slightly for 3 minutes. Stir in the apples and cook until golden, about 12 minutes.

Place the bread cubes in a large bowl and mix with the apple-and-onion mixture, stirring thoroughly. In a small bowl, toss the cranberries with the sugar and lemon zest and mix into the bread cubes. Add the 1 cup cider or juice, parsley, sage, and salt and pepper to taste. The stuffing should be moist but not wet. If it's too dry, add up to ½ cup cider.

Mustard Sauce

½–¾	cup strained drippings from the pork roast or beef stock	⅔	cup Dijon mustard
¾	cup red wine	1¼	cups heavy cream
3	shallots, minced		Sea salt and freshly ground white pepper

Pour the drippings or stock into a small saucepan and add the wine and shallots. Bring to the boiling point over medium heat and simmer over medium-low heat for 20 minutes, stirring occasionally, to reduce the liquid. Add the mustard and cream, return to the boiling point, and immediately reduce the heat and cook, whisking frequently, until the sauce is somewhat thickened, about 10 minutes. Season with salt and pepper to taste. Serve in a sauceboat or pitcher.

OLD-FASHIONED YANKEE POT ROAST

This simple dish requires a tasty cut of meat—there are no embellishments, so each bite stands out. Searing or braising the meat enriches the flavor and takes very little time.

YIELD | 10 SERVINGS

2	tablespoons unsalted butter	1	pound carrots (about 10), trimmed into 2-inch lengths
2	tablespoons canola or safflower oil	½	pound baby bella or shiitake mushrooms, cut in half
1	bottom round roast (about 5-pounds)	1	tablespoon potato starch
2	cups water	½	cup dry red wine
1½	teaspoons salt + more to taste		Freshly ground pepper
1	pound boiling onions, peeled and blanched	¼	cup minced fresh flat-leaf parsley, for garnish
20	red potatoes (about 2 inches in diameter), a strip peeled like a belt around the middle		

In a Dutch oven, heat the butter and oil over medium-high heat and sear the meat on all sides, about 2 minutes per side. Add the water and the 1½ teaspoons salt and bring to the boiling point. Add the onions, potatoes, carrots, and mushrooms, then cover, lower the heat, and simmer until the meat is tender, 2 to 2½ hours. Remove the roast to a cutting board and cover it loosely with foil so it doesn't lose too much heat.

In a small bowl, mix the potato starch with the wine until dissolved. Pour into the Dutch oven and cook over low heat, stirring gently, until it thickens a bit, about 10 minutes. Season with salt and pepper to taste.

To serve the dish: Slice the meat and transfer it to a warm platter. Using a slotted spoon, mound the vegetables on the roast, then ladle the gravy over all. Garnish with the parsley and serve.

POTLUCK NOTE | *To transport this dish, cool the roast when it is cooked. Cover. To serve, slice the beef on a baking dish that you can serve from. Top with the vegetables and sauce and heat in a 350°F oven for 20 minutes.*

FISH AND SHELLFISH

THE EARLIEST DOCUMENTED fish recipe, written in China, dates from 1500 BCE. Around the Mediterranean Sea, the Etruscans had a sophisticated aquacultural system, and Scandinavia claims to have records of cooked fish that go back 4,000 years. All over the world in all societies, fish has been caught, sometimes farmed, dried, smoked, salted, frozen—and always eaten. So jump right in and give it a try. This is your chance, because when you are potlucking, you have only one dish to focus on.

You will be rewarded because fish dishes are always well received. Both delicious and healthy, the recipes in this chapter will deliver dishes that are sure to make your reputation as a fabulous "potlucker."

Fish should never, ever smell fishy—it should never look iridescent or feel slimy. It is best not to buy fish more than a day before you are going to cook it. The best way to buy fish is from a market that has someone to talk to so that if you're uncertain what to buy, you can ask for help. Fish vendors are usually well informed.

Very little special equipment is needed. You don't need a lot of serving dishes— just one or two 13-by-9-inch baking pans that can go from oven to refrigerator to table. A large spatula will help lift and turn fillets without breaking them. Olive oil spray is a great convenience to keep fish from sticking. You can buy it ready to go or buy a refillable spray bottle, which you can fill with your favorite oil.

MARYLAND ROCKFISH CHOWDER

There are several species of fish called rockfish, but in Maryland, "rockfish" is another name for striped bass. The Maryland Watermen's Association holds a rockfishing tournament in Rock Hall, Maryland, each year. It seems that everyone in Rock Hall has a version of this dish.

YIELD | 12 SERVINGS

8	tablespoons (½ cup) unsalted butter
2	cups finely diced onion
2	ribs celery, finely diced
2	pounds Maryland rockfish fillets or other firm whitefish, cut into cubes
8	cups (two 1-quart containers) homemade vegetable stock or canned stock
1	can (28 ounces) diced tomatoes
2	bottles (8 ounces each) clam juice

1	cup white wine (optional)
1½	pounds new potatoes, peeled and cubed
3	cups fresh or frozen corn kernels
2	cups finely diced carrots
2	teaspoons Old Bay seasoning, or to taste
1	teaspoon dried thyme
	Salt and pepper
⅓	cup minced fresh flat-leaf parsley, for garnish

In a Dutch oven or heavy soup pot over medium heat, melt the butter and cook the onion, celery, and fish until browned, about 10 minutes.

One by one, add all the remaining ingredients except the parsley, stirring gently. Bring to a boil, lower the heat, and simmer, uncovered, for 30 minutes.

To serve the dish: Pour the soup into a warmed tureen and garnish with the parsley. Rockfish chowder is usually served with oyster crackers, but hot biscuits are also traditional.

CRAB CAKES WITH REMOULADE SAUCE

These are the real deal and a real treat. Unlike salmon cakes, which are better prepared with canned fish, crab cakes are best made with fresh crabmeat.

YIELD | 10 SERVINGS

1	large egg		Juice of ½ lemon
1	tablespoon mayonnaise		Salt and pepper
½	teaspoon Dijon mustard	1	cup medium-grind cornmeal
1	teaspoon Worcestershire sauce	4	tablespoons (¼ cup) unsalted butter
1	pound backfin crabmeat		
2–3	teaspoons Old Bay seasoning	4	tablespoons olive oil
	Pinch of baking powder		Remoulade Sauce (recipe follows), for serving
25	unsalted saltines, coarsely crumbled		

In a large bowl, mix the egg, mayonnaise, mustard, and Worcestershire sauce. With a fork, toss the crabmeat lightly with the mayonnaise mixture. Stir in the Old Bay seasoning (to taste) and baking powder, then fold in the crackers and lemon juice. Lightly season with salt and pepper to taste.

Form the mixture into 10 (20 for a buffet) patties. Press just hard enough to hold each crab cake together. Pour the cornmeal into a shallow bowl and gently coat each cake.

At this point, if you are planning to cook the crab cakes in another kitchen, layer them with waxed paper in a flat plastic container, cover, and refrigerate for up to 24 hours.

In a large (preferably cast-iron) skillet, heat the butter and oil over medium heat until there is a slight sizzle. Cook the crab cakes until crisp and browned, 4 to 5 minutes per side. Drain on paper towels and serve immediately.

To serve the dish: These are best served within an hour of making. If you cannot do this, cool them on a wire rack for 15 minutes. Layer with parchment or waxed paper in a shallow pan, cover with foil, and refrigerate for up to 24 hours. Heat on one or two baking sheets in a 400°F oven for 10 minutes. Serve hot on a platter with cold Remoulade Sauce in a bowl alongside.

(continued)

Remoulade Sauce

2	large egg yolks	½	cup minced celery
¾	cup olive oil	½	cup minced scallions
½	teaspoon Tabasco	¼	cup capers, minced
1	teaspoon Dijon mustard	¼	teaspoon sweet paprika
2	teaspoons fresh lemon juice		Salt and pepper

Whisk the egg yolks in a small deep bowl, using a balloon whisk. Continue whisking vigorously as you slowly and steadily dribble in the oil. In a few minutes, the mixture will achieve the consistency of mayonnaise. Incorporate the remaining ingredients, place in a covered container, and refrigerate immediately until ready to use.

When serving, do not leave at room temperature for more than 2 hours.

POTLUCK NOTE | *For recipes that call for eggs that are raw or undercooked when the dish is served, use either shell eggs that have been treated to destroy salmonella by pasteurization or another approved method, or pasteurized egg products. Treated shell eggs are available from a growing number of retailers and are clearly labeled.*

POACHED COD WITH LEMON–CAPER BUTTER SAUCE

This melt-in-your-mouth dish is only as good as the fish it is made with. It is very easy to make and to eat. It is especially good accompanied by White Beans with Gremolata (page 74).

YIELD | 10 SERVINGS

Fish

1½	quarts water	¼	teaspoon whole cloves
	Juice of 2 lemons	1	teaspoon coarse salt
1	medium to large onion, sliced	3	pounds cod fillets
¼	teaspoon black peppercorns		

Sauce

1	cup sweet unsalted butter		Finely grated zest of 1 lemon (see page 262)
⅓	cup small capers, rinsed and drained	⅓	cup minced fresh flat-leaf parsley, for garnish
	Juice of 2 medium lemons		

To make the fish: In a large Dutch oven or other pan with a large circumference, bring the water, lemon juice, onion, peppercorns, cloves, and salt to a boil over medium-high heat. Simmer for 10 minutes. Add the cod gently with a slotted spatula. Lower the heat to medium, and simmer until the fish flakes easily with a fork, about 10 to 12 minutes.

To make the sauce: Melt the butter in a saucepan over medium-low heat. Stir in the capers. Reduce the heat to low and slowly stir in the lemon juice. Do not boil. Remove from the heat and stir in the lemon zest.

To serve the dish: Serve the poached cod on a warm platter, topped with the sauce, garnished with the parsley, and accompanied by White Beans with Gremolata served alongside in a warm bowl.

SPANISH-STYLE PAN-ROASTED RED SNAPPER WITH PAN-ROASTED POTATOES

Any green salad in the Salads chapter makes a good accompaniment to this dish.

YIELD | 10 SERVINGS

¼	cup olive oil	1	cup pimiento-stuffed Spanish olives + more for garnish
1½	cups diced sweet onion		
1	large bell pepper, diced	10	red snapper fillets (5 ounces each)
1	pound white mushrooms, sliced	1	teaspoon dried rosemary
1	cup whole blanched almonds (optional)	½	cup fresh orange juice
		½	cup fresh lemon juice
1	cup oil-soaked sun-dried tomatoes, drained and coarsely chopped, homemade or from a jar	½	cup chopped fresh flat-leaf parsley + sprigs for garnish
			Pan-Roasted Potatoes (recipe follows), for serving
½	teaspoon coarse salt		
¼	teaspoon ground white pepper		
½	teaspoon crushed red pepper flakes		

Preheat the oven to 400°F. Spray a 13-by-9-inch dish with olive oil. Heat the oil in a heavy skillet over medium heat. Add the onion and bell pepper and sauté until the onion is golden brown, about 7 minutes. Add the mushrooms and almonds and cook, stirring, until the almonds are golden brown, about 3 minutes. Lower the heat and stir in the tomatoes, salt, white pepper, red pepper flakes, and the 1 cup olives. Mix well and remove from the heat.

Spread half of the vegetable mixture on the bottom of the prepared baking dish. Set the fish fillets on top in a single layer, sprinkle with the rosemary, and pour over the orange and lemon juices, and sprinkle with chopped parsley. Cover with the remaining vegetable mixture. Roast until the fish flakes easily with a fork, 20 to 30 minutes.

To serve the dish: Serve in the baking dish or on a deep, warm serving platter, garnished with the parsley sprigs and additional olives. Serve the Pan-Roasted Potatoes alongside.

(continued)

To prepare the tomatoes yourself, place 1 cup sun-dried tomatoes in a small saucepan and cover with olive oil. Heat over medium-low heat just to a simmer. Remove from the heat and soak overnight. Drain the tomatoes and use. Refrigerate the oil in a covered container for another use, such as salad dressing. Use within a week.

Pan-Roasted Potatoes

YIELD | 10 SIDE-DISH SERVINGS

2½	pounds new potatoes, scrubbed and cut in half	½–1	teaspoon Spanish paprika or other sweet paprika, or to taste
¾	teaspoon salt	1	teaspoon dried rosemary

Preheat the oven to 400°F. Spray a 13-by-9-inch baking dish with olive oil.

Place the potatoes in the prepared baking dish and spray them with additional oil. Season with the salt, paprika, and rosemary and roast until crisp and fork-tender, 40 to 45 minutes.

If you are serving this dish immediately, you can place the potatoes in the preheated oven while you are sautéing the ingredients for the snapper.

POTLUCK NOTE | *Although, like all fish dishes, this is best served immediately, it is sturdy enough to be cooled, covered, and refrigerated for 24 hours and reheated before serving. Heat in a 425°F oven for 10 minutes. The same is true of the potatoes.*

FILLET OF FISH EN PAPILLOTE

"En papillote" is the French term for food baked in parchment paper (more literally, "curled paper"). As the fish cooks, it steams in its own juices. This is a terrific potluck dish because you can make the fish packets, then refrigerate them for several hours before placing them on a baking sheet in a pre-heated oven. Everyone likes opening packages, so this dish is sure to please.

YIELD | 10 SERVINGS

10	circles (12 inches in diameter) of parchment paper	1	sweet onion, julienned
10	small new potatoes, peeled and sliced paper-thin	2	zucchini, julienned
10	sea trout (weakfish) or orange roughy fillets (4–6 ounces each)	5	plum tomatoes, sliced lengthwise
		2	teaspoons dried thyme
			Salt and pepper

Preheat the oven to 400°F.

Lay out the circles of parchment on a work surface. Fold each in half to make a crease, then open them up again. Spray with olive oil. As you proceed, keep all ingredients on one half of the circle and leave a 1-inch border around the edge.

Divide the potatoes evenly and fan them out on each half circle. Top with the fish, then add the onion and zucchini. Top with the tomatoes, thyme, and salt and pepper to taste. Fold each circle in half over the filling and, starting at one end, fold over the edges of the paper two or three times to seal the packets. Press tightly so juices don't leak out. You can place a few paper clips around the edges; just make sure to remove them before serving.

At this point you can refrigerate the fish packets for several hours.

Place the packets on two baking sheets and bake until the fish flakes easily with a fork, about 20 minutes.

To serve the dish: Serve immediately on individual plates or a large platter. If the packets are going to sit on a buffet table, cut a slit in each one to allow the steam to escape and stop the cooking.

SALMON BURGERS WITH ONION JAM

YIELD | 10 SALMON BURGERS

3½	pounds salmon fillet, skinned
1½	cups finely diced red onion
1½	cups finely diced red bell pepper
¼	cup minced fresh flat-leaf parsley
2	cups fine fresh bread crumbs
	Juice of 1 lemon
1	teaspoon dried thyme
½	teaspoon dried rosemary

Freshly ground black pepper

3 egg whites, beaten until foamy but not stiff

Safflower oil, for sautéing

Onion Jam (recipe follows), for serving

10 hamburger rolls, toasted

Pick out all the bones from the salmon, cut it into 4-inch pieces, and mince with a sharp 8-inch chef's knife. Alternatively, pulse the fish a few pieces at a time in a food processor fitted with the metal blade. Do not turn the fish into mush.

In a large bowl, combine the salmon with the onion, bell pepper, parsley, and bread crumbs, then stir in the lemon juice, thyme, and rosemary. Season with black pepper to taste. Fold in the egg whites. Shape into 10 patties about ¾ inch thick. You can prepare burgers 12 hours in advance and keep them covered with plastic wrap in a single layer in the refrigerator.

On a griddle or in a large skillet brushed heavily with safflower oil, sauté the burgers in a single layer over medium-high heat until cooked through and golden brown on both sides, about 4 minutes per side. Repeat until all the burgers are cooked.

To serve the dish: Serve immediately, with the Onion Jam and toasted burger rolls. Or place the cooked burgers on a baking sheet and keep warm in a 200°F oven until ready to serve, up to 20 minutes.

Onion Jam

YIELD | 4 CUPS

3	tablespoons unsalted butter	¼	cup sugar
3	tablespoons extra-virgin olive oil	½	teaspoon ground allspice
10	medium to large onions, sliced and separated into rings	1½	cups red wine

Heat the butter and oil in a large sauté pan over medium heat. Add the onions and sauté for 4 minutes, or until transparent. Stir in the sugar and allspice, then lower the heat and stir in the wine. Cook, stirring frequently, until all the liquid has been absorbed, about 20 minutes. Onion Jam can be cooled, covered, and refrigerated for up to 3 days.

PAN-ROASTED SALMON WITH MINT PESTO

I am a salmon enthusiast because the fish is flavorful on its own, yet can stand up to strong seasonings and rich sauces. This dish is a springtime favorite—fresh mint is abundant then—but you can make it anytime. If you plan to serve it at a buffet or a light lunch, cut the salmon fillets in half.

YIELD | 10 SERVINGS

1	cup extra-virgin olive oil	¼	teaspoon coarse salt
4–5	cloves garlic, roughly chopped		Mint sprigs, for garnish
1	cup fresh mint leaves, large stems removed, and 1 tablespoon dried mint	12	salmon fillets (5 ounces each)
1½	cups toasted broken walnuts		Sea salt and freshly ground pepper

Preheat the oven to 360°F.

To make the pesto: Place ¾ cup of the oil, garlic, mint leaves, and dried mint in a small food processor and puree, but don't liquefy. Add the walnuts and salt and pulse until finely chopped. The pesto can be made 24 hours in advance, covered, and refrigerated. Bring to room temperature before spreading on the salmon.

To make the salmon: Pour the remaining ¼ cup oil in a 13-by-17-inch rimmed baking sheet, large enough to hold the salmon in one layer. Spread the pesto on the salmon fillets. Roast for 20 minutes. If possible, place the salmon under the broiler for the last 2 minutes of cooking time before serving.

To serve the dish: Serve from the baking sheet or, with the aid of a slotted spatula, place the pesto-topped fillets on a platter. Garnish with the mint sprigs, and offer sea salt and a pepper mill. Bow-tie pasta tossed with oil, garlic, and toasted walnuts makes a nice accompaniment.

POTLUCK NOTE | *To toast walnuts, spread them on a rimmed baking sheet and bake in a 400°F oven for 7 to 10 minutes, turning with a spatula after 4 minutes, until fragrant and lightly toasted.*

STIR-FRIED RICE WITH MUSHROOMS AND SHRIMP

This flexible dish incorporates a lot of precooked ingredients, and it is surprisingly delicious; each mouthful tastes a little different from the last. Cooked beef, pork, and/or chicken can be added or substituted for the shrimp, and it can be made with white or brown rice.

YIELD | 10 BUFFET SERVINGS

4	tablespoons peanut oil	¾	pound mushrooms, sliced
1	tablespoon grated fresh ginger	1	pound cooked large (24–30 per pound) shrimp
6	scallions, minced		
4	eggs, lightly whisked with 2 tablespoons water	2	cans (12 ounces) baby corn, drained and rinsed
3	cloves garlic, minced	⅓	cup light soy sauce or tamari
1	red bell pepper, seeded and cut in lengthwise strips	1	tablespoon sugar
		1	tablespoon sesame oil
7½	cups cooked white or brown rice		

Heat 2 tablespoons of the peanut oil in a wok or large sauté pan. Add half of the ginger, half of the scallions, and the eggs and stir until the eggs are just solid. Remove to a plate and set aside. Add the remaining 2 tablespoons peanut oil to the wok and stir in the garlic, the remaining ginger and scallions, and the bell pepper. Cook, stirring, until the scallions are slightly browned, about 3 minutes. Add the rice and cook until the grains are hot and free of clumps. Push the rice to the side of the wok, stir in the mushrooms and shrimp, stir in the corn, and cook until the shrimp are heated through, 3 to 4 minutes longer. Add the reserved cooked eggs and stir until broken up. Add the soy sauce or tamari, sugar, and sesame oil and mix well.

To serve the dish: Place in a warm serving bowl and serve with a deep serving spoon.

POTLUCK NOTE | *Cooked rice stays fresh refrigerated, tightly covered, for up to 1 week or frozen up to 6 months. To heat, add 2 tablespoons of liquid per cup of rice. Cover and heat about 5 minutes on top of the stove, or microwave on high about 1 minute per cup of rice.*

SHRIMP COCONUT CURRY WITH BASMATI RICE

A long time ago in a galaxy far, far away, I lived on the Spanish island of Ibiza for a year. Our neighbors, an Indian/French couple, cooked the most exotic dishes I had ever tasted from a home kitchen. This is only one of a variety of a seafood curries that we made and ate. You can personalize it after you have made it once or twice.

YIELD | 10 TO 12 SERVINGS

¼	cup clarified butter (see page 262) or canola oil	4	medium to large onions, sliced
1	piece (2 inches) fresh ginger, minced	3	pounds ripe tomatoes, diced, or 2 cans (28 ounces each) diced tomatoes, drained
6	cloves garlic, minced	2	cups unsweetened coconut milk
1–2	green, slightly hot chili peppers, such as Anaheim or poblano (ask your produce manager), seeded and thinly sliced, or to taste (optional)	3	pounds extra-large shrimp (25–30 per pound), peeled and deveined
2	tablespoons Madras curry powder	1½	cups shredded coconut
1	teaspoon ground cardamom	½	cup minced fresh cilantro, for garnish
1	teaspoon ground cumin	1	cup toasted coconut (see page 262), for garnish (optional)
1	teaspoon ground coriander		Basmati Rice (recipe follows), for serving
2	tablespoons packed dark brown sugar		

Heat the ghee or oil in a large skillet over medium-low heat. With a wooden spoon, stir in the ginger, garlic, chili peppers, curry powder, cardamom, cumin, and coriander and cook until aromatic, 2 to 3 minutes. Stir in the sugar and onions and sauté until the onions are golden brown, about 7 minutes. Stir in the tomatoes and coconut milk and cook, stirring until the mixture comes to a low boil, 7 to 8 minutes. Stir in the shrimp and cook, stirring constantly, for 5 to 7 minutes. Do not overcook or the shrimp will be tough. Stir in the shredded coconut and remove from the heat.

To serve the dish: Transfer to a deep serving platter and top with the cilantro and, if you like, toasted coconut. Set a bowl of hot Basmati Rice alongside. Indian breads and Peach Chutney (page 92) are also good accompaniments.

Basmati Rice

YIELD | 8 CUPS

3	tablespoons clarified butter (see page 262) or unsalted butter	7	cups water + 1 cup more, if needed
4	cups basmati rice, rinsed in several changes of water and drained	¾	teaspoon salt (optional)

Heat the butter in a large heavy-bottomed pot with a tight-fitting lid over medium-high heat. Add the rice and stir for a few minutes, until it is shiny and almost translucent. Stir in the 7 cups water and bring to a boil. Stir in the salt. Cover, lower the heat, and simmer until the rice is tender, about 20 minutes. Check the rice after 15 minutes and add more water if the rice is cooking dry. Remove from the heat, transfer to a warm serving bowl, and fluff with a fork.

The rice can be made a day before serving. Line a large colander with cheesecloth, leaving enough overhang to cover the rice. Place the rice in the colander, cover with the cheesecloth, and cool. Refrigerate, covered with foil or plastic wrap. When ready to serve, remove the wrap and set the colander in a large covered pot with 2 inches of simmering water. Heat for 10 minutes, turn out in a warm serving bowl, and fluff with a fork.

TILAPIA FAJITAS WITH TOMATO SALSA, CHIPOTLE CREAM, AND GUACAMOLE

What delicious fun these are! They're even more fun with a margarita.

YIELD | 12 SERVINGS (2 FAJITAS EACH)

3	pounds tilapia fillets, cut into strips	½	scant teaspoon garlic powder
¼	teaspoon freshly ground black pepper + more to taste		Juice of 1 orange
			Juice of 1 lime
½	teaspoon salt + more to taste	3	tablespoons extra-virgin olive oil
½	teaspoon ground cumin	1	large sweet onion, halved lengthwise and sliced
1	teaspoon ancho chili powder		
1	teaspoon dried oregano	2	green bell peppers, seeded and sliced
	Dash of cayenne pepper (optional)	1	red bell pepper, seeded and sliced

Accompaniments

24	soft flour tortillas (6 inches in diameter)	Tomato Salsa, Chipotle Cream, and Guacamole (recipes follow), for serving
2	cups shredded cheddar cheese	
3	cups shredded lettuce	
2	limes, cut in thin wedges	

Place the tilapia in an 8-by-8-inch baking dish. In a bowl, mix the ¼ teaspoon black pepper, the ½ teaspoon salt, cumin, chili powder, oregano, cayenne pepper (if using), garlic powder, and citrus juices and pour over the fish. Cover with plastic wrap and refrigerate for 30 to 45 minutes (no longer). Turn the fish once or twice.

Heat the oil in a large skillet over medium heat. Add the onion and bell peppers and sauté until the onions are golden brown, about 7 minutes. Season with salt and black pepper to taste. Remove the vegetables with a slotted spoon and reserve.

(continued)

Transfer the tilapia from the marinade to the skillet and sauté gently until the fish flakes easily with a fork, about 4 minutes per side. Return the onion and peppers to the skillet and stir.

Wrap the tortillas in foil (two stacks of 12 each) and heat in a 200°F oven or toaster oven for 5 minutes.

To serve the dish: Transfer the fish and vegetables to a deep serving platter and serve immediately with the tortillas, cheese, lettuce, and limes. Serve bowls of Tomato Salsa, Chipotle Cream, and Guacamole alongside so people can make their own fajitas.

Tomato Salsa

YIELD | ABOUT 2½ CUPS

1	large red onion, finely chopped		Juice of 1 orange
3	large ripe tomatoes, finely chopped		Juice of 1 lime
		⅓	cup chopped fresh cilantro
1	clove garlic, minced		Salt and freshly ground black pepper
2	green chili peppers, seeded and finely chopped, or 1 can (4 ounces) chopped green chili peppers		

In a large bowl, using a wooden spoon, mix all the ingredients by hand, crushing them together. It is better not to use a blender, as the salsa will get too mushy. Cover and refrigerate until ready to serve, up to 24 hours.

Chipotle Cream

YIELD | ABOUT 3½ CUPS

16   ounces (2 cups) regular or light sour cream

1   cup regular or light mayonnaise

⅓   cup sweet pickle relish, drained

⅓   cup minced shallots

¼   cup chopped fresh cilantro

1   tablespoon minced chipotle chili peppers, or to taste

In a large bowl, mix all the ingredients, cover, and refrigerate until ready to use, for up to 24 hours.

Guacamole

YIELD | ABOUT 3 CUPS

3   ripe avocados

   Juice of 2 limes

   Grated zest of ½ lime (see page 262)

3   cloves garlic, finely minced

½   cup finely minced sweet or red onion

3   tablespoons chopped fresh cilantro

1 or 2   serrano chili peppers, seeded and minced, or to taste

¼   teaspoon sea salt, or to taste

Peel, pit, and slice the avocados and place them in a medium mixing bowl. Mash with a fork and add the lime juice, lime zest, garlic, onion, cilantro, and chili peppers. Season with salt to taste.

POTLUCK NOTE | *Cooks in Mexico and other parts of the world mash avocados in a molcajete, a basalt mortar and pestle. If you make guacamole a lot, it's a good kitchen tool to have. It's also useful for making pesto, aioli, and other compound sauces. You can serve from it as well.*

VEGETABLES

POTLUCK EVENTS are the perfect occasions to fuss with vegetables, which are so often treated as an afterthought. Remember that you are making only one dish—so go for it. Julia Child once said that she thought the reason many people didn't like vegetables was because they were cooked like medicine. These recipes are anything but, and will get as many oohs and aahs as any dish on the table.

They are all from scratch because these days, almost every market has good-quality vegetables year-round. Generally speaking, if you do need (or want) to substitute, frozen products are better than canned. Fresh herbs have also become available in almost surprising abundance. If you need to buy more than a recipe calls for, freeze the remainder in a freezer bag, pushing out as much air as you can before sealing.

No special equipment is needed, but a good vegetable peeler and a mandoline with a metal blade are very useful. And, because many of the dishes are prepared in the oven, a 13-by-9-inch oven-to-table baking dish is essential. A comparably sized, covered plastic insulated container is also helpful for storing and transporting dishes. An 8-inch chef's knife, a small sharp paring knife, and a bird's beak knife will help you make almost anything here. Two colanders are useful for washing and draining.

There are other vegetable recipes scattered throughout the book as accompaniments and side dishes for other recipes, so check the index for additional choices.

STUFFED ZUCCHINI

YIELD | 10 SIDE-DISH SERVINGS

10	small/medium zucchini (uniform in size, about 3 pounds total)	2	cups freshly grated Parmigiano-Reggiano cheese
	Salt and pepper	½–1	cup dry bread crumbs
3	eggs, lightly beaten		

Preheat the oven to 425°F. Spray a baking sheet with oil.

In a large pot of boiling water, cook the zucchini until fork-tender, about 7 minutes. With a slotted spoon, transfer the zucchini to a bowl of ice water to stop the cooking. Leave in the water for 3 minutes. Remove and pat dry with paper towels.

Halve the zucchini lengthwise and scoop out the pulp, leaving a ⅓-inch-thick shell. Sprinkle the shells with salt and pepper and turn them upside down on paper towels to drain.

Squeeze the pulp dry and place in a food processor fitted with the metal blade. Add the eggs, cheese, and bread crumbs and pulse two or three times. Do not turn it into paste.

Wipe the zucchini shells dry, turn them cut side up, and fill with the zucchini mixture. For a decorative finish, use a pastry bag to fill the shells.

Place the stuffed zucchini on the prepared baking sheet and bake until golden brown and a bit puffed, about 17 minutes. At this point, if you are not serving them immediately, they can be cooled, covered, and refrigerated for up to 24 hours.

To serve the dish: Serve warm or at room temperature. If the zucchini have been made ahead and refrigerated, warm them in a 300°F oven for 15 minutes.

TOMATOES PROVENÇALE

This easy-to-make recipe is especially refreshing.

YIELD | 10 SIDE-DISH SERVINGS

10	tomatoes (uniform in size)	4	cloves garlic, minced
	Up to ½ cup extra-virgin olive oil	¾	cup fine dry bread crumbs
	Salt and pepper to taste		
½	cup chopped fresh flat-leaf parsley		

Preheat the oven to 400°F. Brush or spray one or two baking dishes or a larger roasting pan with olive oil.

Wash the tomatoes and cut off the top one-third of each tomato. Cut out the tough cores and discard.

Place the tomatoes cut side up in the prepared dish(es). Drizzle with ¼ cup of the oil and season lightly with salt and pepper. Roast for 10 minutes.

In a small bowl, mix the parsley, garlic, and bread crumbs.

Remove the tomatoes from the oven, brush with some or all of the remaining ¼ cup oil, and top each with the bread-crumb mixture. Return to the oven for 5 minutes, or until the topping is slightly browned. At this point, the tomatoes can be cooled, covered with plastic wrap, and refrigerated for up to 24 hours.

To serve the dish: If you've made the tomatoes and refrigerated them, heat them in a 250°F oven for 15 minutes and serve hot or at room temperature.

SAUTÉED BROCCOLI WITH GARLIC

YIELD | 10 SIDE-DISH SERVINGS

2½	pounds broccoli	½	teaspoon sea salt
¼	cup extra-virgin olive oil	¼	cup minced fresh flat-leaf parsley
6	cloves garlic, minced		

Trim the tough ends of the broccoli and pare the thick skin on the stalks. Cut each stalk into several stems and rinse.

Bring a large pot of water to a boil and blanch the broccoli for 5 minutes. Drain. The blanched broccoli can be cooled and refrigerated until you're ready to serve. It may take a little longer to sauté if it's cold.

Heat the oil in a large skillet over medium-high heat. Stir in the garlic and as soon as it sizzles, add the broccoli. Cook, stirring, until the broccoli is fork-tender, about 10 minutes. Stir in the salt and parsley.

To serve the dish: Transfer the broccoli to a serving bowl and serve hot.

GREEK-STYLE GREEN POLE BEANS

YIELD | 10 TO 12 SIDE-DISH SERVINGS

2½	pounds green pole beans, rinsed, strings and stem ends removed		Grated zest of ½ lemon
4	plum tomatoes, diced		Salt and pepper
3	tablespoons extra-virgin olive oil	⅔	cup coarsely chopped toasted hazelnuts (optional)
	Juice of ½ lemon		

Bring a large pot of water to a boil and boil the beans for 5 minutes, or until cooked but crunchy—taste one, as they vary. Drain. In a large serving bowl, toss the beans with the tomatoes, oil, and lemon juice. Stir in the lemon zest and salt and pepper to taste. Top with the hazelnuts, if desired.

To serve the dish: Serve hot or at room temperature.

CAULIFLOWER WITH OLIVE OIL AND LEMON

YIELD | 10 SIDE-DISH SERVINGS

1	large head cauliflower or 2 small	½	teaspoon freshly grated or ground nutmeg
⅓	cup extra-virgin olive oil + more for greasing	½	teaspoon sea salt
	Juice of 1½ lemons		Freshly ground pepper to taste

Preheat the oven to 400°F. Spray a large foil-lined baking dish with oil.

Rinse and drain the cauliflower. Cut off the thick stems and trim the leaves. Separate into 2-inch florets. Place in a single layer in the prepared baking dish and drizzle with the ⅓ cup oil and lemon juice. Sprinkle with the nutmeg and salt and season with pepper to taste. Roast, turning occasionally, until fork-tender, about 20 minutes.

To serve the dish: Transfer the cauliflower to a platter and serve hot or at room temperature.

POTLUCK NOTE | *Cauliflower is very pretty when steamed or simmered whole, but it's difficult to serve to a crowd. If you want to give it a try, bring two pots of water to a boil and simmer two 8-inch cauliflowers, trimmed of leaves and stems so they can stand upright on their own. Cook until fork-tender, about 30 minutes. Drain, stand on platters, and top with lemon juice, oil, and seasoning.*

SWEET-AND-SOUR RED CABBAGE AND APPLES

This tasty side dish makes a bright accompaniment to ham. It can be made several days before it is needed.

YIELD | 10 SIDE-DISH SERVINGS

3	tablespoons unsalted butter	½	cup packed brown sugar
1	head red cabbage (2 pounds), cored and shredded	½	red wine vinegar
		⅔	cup red currant jelly
4	apples, such as McIntosh or Empire, cored and thinly sliced	½	cup sweet wine, such as port + more if needed
½	teaspoon salt		

In a Dutch oven or other large heavy-bottomed saucepan with a cover, melt the butter over medium heat and stir in the cabbage and apples. Stir in the salt, brown sugar, and vinegar. Add the jelly and wine. Bring to the boiling point, then cover, lower the heat, and simmer for 20 minutes. Stir occasionally and add more wine if the mixture seems too dry.

If not serving immediately, let cool, cover, and refrigerate for up to 2 days.

To serve the dish: If you've made the dish ahead of time, heat it over medium heat for 10 minutes, or until hot. Place in a deep serving bowl with a deep serving spoon.

ROASTED GARLIC MASHED POTATOES

2½ pounds russet potatoes, peeled
    and held in a bowl of cold water

1   teaspoon coarse salt + more to
    taste

6   tablespoons unsalted butter,
    sliced, at room temperature

1   head roasted garlic, removed
    from skin and mashed
    (see page 262)

⅓   cup heavy cream

⅔   cup milk

    Few turns of a pepper mill

½   teaspoon nutmeg (optional)

Cut the potatoes into 2-inch chunks and place in a large pot of cold water with the 1 teaspoon salt over medium-high heat. Boil uncovered for 20 minutes or until a piece is easily broken with a fork.

Drain the potatoes and place them in a bowl large enough to hold all the ingredients. Mash the potatoes with a fork; then, using an electric handheld mixer, mash with the butter, garlic, cream, and ⅓ cup milk. Add more of the remaining ⅓ cup milk, if necessary, and season with salt, pepper, and nutmeg (if desired) to taste. Serve immediately or cool, cover, and refrigerate, for up to 24 hours.

POTLUCK NOTE | *The potatoes can be made a day in advance and heated in the top of a double boiler or in a shallow baking dish covered with foil in a 350°F oven for 15 minutes.*

SWEET POTATO CASSEROLE WITH PECAN TOPPING

The sweet potato is indigenous to the Americas, as is the pecan. George Washington grew sweet potatoes at Mount Vernon, and variations of this dish have been made and eaten for hundreds of years.

YIELD | 10 SIDE-DISH SERVINGS

Potatoes

4	pounds sweet potatoes (4 or 5), scrubbed	1	teaspoon ground nutmeg
10	tablespoons unsalted butter, sliced, at room temperature	1	teaspoon ground cinnamon
½	cup packed brown sugar	½	teaspoon ground ginger
½	cup molasses	½	cup bourbon (optional)
			Salt and pepper to taste

Topping

½	cup packed light brown sugar	6	tablespoons unsalted butter, melted
½	cup packed dark brown sugar	2	cups broken pecans
½	cup cream		

To make the potatoes: Place the potatoes in a large pot of water, bring to a boil, and boil for 40 minutes, or until fork-tender. Drain and let cool.

Preheat the oven to 350°F. Spray a 13-by-9-inch baking dish with olive oil.

When they are cool enough to handle, peel the sweet potatoes and transfer to a large bowl. Mash, then stir in the butter, sugar, molasses, nutmeg, cinnamon, and ginger. Stir in the bourbon, if using, and season with salt and pepper to taste. Place in the prepared baking dish, and use a rubber spatula to spread it end to end and make some decorative swirls. At this point, the dish can be cooled, covered, and refrigerated for up to 2 days.

To make the topping: In a small bowl, mix the sugars together and sprinkle over the sweet potatoes. Drizzle the cream and butter over all and top with the pecans.

Bake until the sugar has caramelized, about 30 minutes.

To serve the dish: Serve hot, directly from the baking dish.

OVEN-ROASTED ROOT VEGETABLES

YIELD | 10 SIDE-DISH SERVINGS

6 tablespoons extra-virgin olive oil

2 teaspoons coarse salt

Freshly ground pepper

1 celery root (about 1 pound), peeled and cut into large dice

3 carrots, scraped and cut into large dice

4 parsnips, scraped and cut into large dice

1½ pounds small potatoes, peeled and cut into large dice

10 small shallots, peeled and halved

2 tablespoons fresh thyme

A few sprigs fresh thyme or ¼ cup chopped flat-leaf parsley, for garnish (optional)

Preheat the oven to 425°F.

Place the oil, salt, and pepper to taste in a large bowl. Add all the vegetables and stir to coat with the seasoned oil.

If you are preparing this dish in another kitchen, you can transfer the oiled vegetables to a large plastic bag and carry the thyme in another small bag. Bring along two baking sheets and proceed at your destination.

Spread the vegetables on the baking sheets and roast, stirring occasionally, until well browned and fork-tender, about 45 minutes. Sprinkle with the thyme and mix. Roast for 2 to 3 minutes more.

These can be carried in a covered container and served warm at your destination. If you prefer them hot, heat in a single layer on a baking sheet in a 350°F oven for 6 to 8 minutes.

To serve the dish: Transfer the roasted vegetables to a serving platter and serve immediately. Garnish with the thyme sprigs or chopped parsley, if desired.

TWICE-BAKED POTATOES

Among the most welcome sides at a potluck are these very easy-to-make, satisfying potatoes.

YIELD | 10 SIDE-DISH SERVINGS

5	baking potatoes (uniform in size), scrubbed and dried	1	tablespoon + 1 teaspoon minced fresh chives
5	tablespoons unsalted butter, sliced, at room-temperature	2	cups grated cheddar cheese
16	ounces (2 cups) regular or light sour cream	6	strips crisp cooked bacon, crumbled, for serving
¼	cup heavy cream	6	scallions, thinly sliced, for serving
	Salt and pepper	16	ounces (2 cups) regular or light sour cream, for serving

Preheat the oven to 375°F.

Pierce the potatoes once or twice with a fork and spray with olive oil. Bake until fork-tender, 45 minutes to 1 hour. Remove from the oven and increase the oven temperature to 400°F.

Cut the potatoes in half lengthwise with a very sharp knife. Gently remove the potato flesh from the skins—leaving ¼ inch of potato attached to the skins to keep them firm—and transfer to a large bowl. Place the potato shells on a baking sheet. With a handheld electric mixer on medium speed, mash the potatoes and beat in the butter, sour cream, and heavy cream. Season with salt and pepper to taste and stir in 1 tablespoon of the chives and 1 cup of the cheese.

Carefully spoon the mixture into the potato shells, mounding the filling slightly in the middle. At this point, the potatoes can be refrigerated in a baking dish or plastic refrigerator container. Place them in a single layer and cover with plastic wrap.

To serve the dish: If serving the potatoes immediately after stuffing, top with the remaining 1 cup of the cheese and bake for 15 minutes, or until they are hot and the cheese is melted. If you've made them a day ahead, bring to room temperature before topping and baking. Serve in individual dessert bowls or from a large buffet platter with small bowls of the chives, bacon, scallions, and sour cream alongside.

POTATO–TURNIP GRATIN

This classic cooking style is suitable for many vegetables, but potatoes are most often used. In a slight twist, this recipe includes turnips as well as potatoes. (You can, of course, substitute additional potatoes for the turnips.) For the best flavor, choose turnips that are no larger than 2 inches across. The trick to this dish is cutting the vegetables uniformly thin. For the dish to bake properly, you want slices that are ¼ inch thick. This is a good time to use a mandoline.

YIELD | 12 SIDE-DISH SERVINGS

6	russet or white potatoes (about 2½ pounds total), scrubbed	¾	teaspoon freshly ground black pepper
6	turnips (about 1½ pounds total), scrubbed	½	teaspoon ground nutmeg
			Dash of cayenne pepper
½	pint (1 cup) cream	1	cup minced shallots
2	cups milk	1	teaspoon sea salt
1½	teaspoons fresh rosemary	1½	cups shredded Gruyère or Swiss cheese
1½	teaspoons fresh thyme		

Preheat the oven to 375°F. Spray a 13-by-9-inch baking dish or gratin baker with olive oil. Peel and cut the potatoes and turnips into ¼-inch-thick slices and place them in a large bowl of cold water.

In a heavy-bottomed saucepan, heat the cream and milk over medium-low heat until simmering. Remove from the heat and stir in the rosemary, thyme, black pepper, nutmeg, and cayenne.

Drain the potatoes and turnips and pat dry with paper towels. In a large bowl, mix the potato and turnip slices with the shallots and salt. Place half of the mixture in the prepared baking dish. Pour half of the cream mixture over the vegetables, then place the remaining vegetables on top of that. Pour the rest of the cream mixture over all and cover with the cheese. At this point, the dish can be covered with plastic wrap and refrigerated for up to 24 hours before baking and serving.

Bake until the vegetables are fork-tender, about 1 hour. If the top is not brown and bubbly, place under the broiler for 3 minutes. Let rest for 10 minutes before serving.

To serve the dish: If you've made the dish ahead, let it return to room temperature before baking. Serve hot, directly from the baking dish.

POTLUCK NOTE | *If you can't get fresh herbs, substitute 1 teaspoon of a dried blend, such as herbes de Provence, for 3 teaspoons of fresh.*

VEGETABLE FRITTATA

I don't know of a country or region that doesn't have a version of this dish.

YIELD | 10 SIDE-DISH SERVINGS

1	pound medium to thin asparagus, tough ends removed		6	extra-large eggs, lightly beaten
3	tablespoons olive oil + more for greasing		4	scallions, thinly sliced and separated into rings
2	russet potatoes, scrubbed and cut into ¼-inch slices			Salt and pepper to taste
6	extra-large egg whites, lightly beaten		½	cup shredded Fontina or Parmigiano-Reggiano cheese

Preheat the oven to 350°F. Spray a 13-by-9-inch oven-to-table baking dish with oil.

In a shallow skillet, bring some water to a boil, add the asparagus, and return to a boil. Lower the heat and simmer until the asparagus are tender, about 3 to 4 minutes. Remove from the water with tongs and drain on paper towels. Cut into 1-inch pieces.

Dry the skillet and heat the 3 tablespoons oil over medium heat. Add the potatoes and cook, turning once or twice, until crisp but not cooked through, about 8 minutes. With a slotted spatula, transfer to the prepared baking dish.

In a small bowl, whisk the egg whites until they are white and foamy but not stiff. In a large bowl, fold the egg whites into the beaten eggs. Stir in the asparagus and scallions. Season with salt and pepper to taste. Pour over the potatoes and top with the cheese.

Bake until the eggs are set and the top is golden brown in spots, about 20 minutes.

To serve the dish: Serve warm or at room temperature directly from the baking dish. This dish can be transported in a thermal container, but it is best not to reheat it because the eggs will get tough.

EGGPLANT PARMIGIANA

This dish has many steps, but don't let that scare you. In kitchens throughout southern Italy, Eggplant Parmigiana is made in many different ways. It is very forgiving and very delicious.

YIELD | 10 SERVINGS

3	pounds (2 or 3 large) eggplants	¾	cup all-purpose flour
	Coarse salt	1	cup fine dry bread crumbs or panko
1	can (28 ounces) crushed tomatoes		
4	ripe tomatoes, peeled, seeded, and diced, or 1 can (28 ounces) whole tomatoes, drained	6	extra-large eggs, beaten
		¼	cup water
4	cloves garlic, minced	1½	pounds mozzarella cheese, cut into ¼-inch-thick slices
⅓	cup olive oil + more for frying (or use canola oil for frying)	2	cups shredded Parmigiano-Reggiano cheese
2	tablespoons sugar	1	cup shredded fresh basil
2	tablespoons balsamic vinegar	1½	cups freshly grated Parmigiano-Reggiano cheese, for serving
1	teaspoon dried oregano		
	Salt and freshly ground pepper		

Cut the eggplants lengthwise into ¼-inch-thick slices and sprinkle both sides with coarse salt. Arrange the slices in layers in one large colander or two regular ones and cover with a heavy plate or pan. Let drain in the sink for 2 hours. This step will assure a good texture to the eggplant.

Place all the tomatoes, garlic, and the ⅓ cup oil in a medium saucepan over medium heat. Add the sugar, vinegar, and oregano, then season with salt and pepper to taste. Stir thoroughly, mashing the tomatoes against the side of the pan. Heat the sauce just to boiling, then stir; remove from the heat, and set aside.

On a baking sheet, combine the flour and bread crumbs or panko and stir with a fork. Lightly beat the eggs and water in an 8-by-8-inch baking dish.

When the eggplant has drained, rinse the slices and press them flat to squeeze out the excess water, then place the slices on paper towels. Dredge the eggplant slices first in the flour mixture and then in the beaten eggs and set on a platter.

Heat 1 inch of oil in a cast-iron or other heavy skillet over medium-high heat until a drop of water sizzles. When the oil is sizzling, fry the eggplant two or three slices at a time until both sides are golden brown, about 3 minutes per side. Use a slotted spatula to turn the slices. Remove to paper towels and continue until all the eggplant is fried. Add more oil, as needed, after a few batches.

Preheat the oven to 350°F.

Oil an oven-to-table 15-by-12-inch baking dish. Spread 1 cup of the sauce over the bottom of the dish. Top with one-third of the eggplant. Cover the eggplant with one-third of the mozzarella and sprinkle with one-third of the shredded Parmigiano-Reggiano and one-third of the basil.

Make a second layer of eggplant, 1 cup sauce, and half of the remaining mozzarella, shredded Parmigiano-Reggiano, and basil. Repeat for the third layer.

Bake until the top is lightly browned, about 35 minutes. Allow to rest at room temperature for at least 10 minutes before serving, to cool and firm slightly.

If you are traveling with this dish, cover it with foil and heat it at your destination. You can also make it a day ahead, refrigerate, and heat.

To serve the dish: If you've made the dish just before going to your event, heat it covered with foil in a 350°F oven for 15 minutes. If you made it the day before, let it come to room temperature first. In either case, remove the foil for the last 5 minutes of heating. Cut into portions with a sharp knife, and serve directly from the baking dish. Serve with crusty Italian bread and the freshly grated Parmigiano-Reggiano.

CARROT–GINGER SOUP

This brightly colored soup perfumes the buffet table. The ingredients are available year-round, so it can be made whenever you like. It also freezes well and, more important, defrosts well.

YIELD | 3 QUARTS (12 ONE-CUP SERVINGS)

4	tablespoons olive oil
2	cups finely chopped sweet onions
2	cloves garlic, minced
2	pounds carrots, finely diced
12	cups vegetable stock
2	tablespoons minced fresh ginger
½	teaspoon salt
½	teaspoon ground ginger
	Juice of 2 sweet oranges

Grated zest of 1 orange

1 tablespoon turbinado or brown sugar

Salt and freshly ground pepper

16 ounces (2 cups) crème fraîche or sour cream, for topping

¼ cup minced crystallized ginger, for garnish (optional)

Heat the oil over medium heat in a Dutch oven or wide heavy-bottomed pot large enough to hold all the ingredients. Add the onions and garlic and sauté until the onions are transparent, about 3 minutes. Add the carrots and cook uncovered, stirring, until slightly softened, about 5 minutes. Add the stock, fresh ginger, salt, and ground ginger. Bring to a boil, lower the heat, stir, and simmer until the carrots are fork-tender, about 45 minutes.

In a covered blender, puree the soup in batches until very smooth. You may want to let the soup cool a bit before putting it in the blender, in case it splashes.

Return the soup to the pot. Add the orange juice, zest, and sugar, and season with salt and pepper to taste. Stir and bring to a high simmer over medium heat. Lower the heat, stir, and simmer gently until the soup is hot throughout, about 3 minutes. Do not let the bottom scorch.

The soup can be cooled, covered, and refrigerated for up to 2 days.

To serve the dish: Serve very hot and offer crème fraîche or sour cream as a topping. Garnish with slivers of crystallized ginger, if desired.

SOUTHWEST VEGETABLE CHILI

This chili is one of the best potluck dishes I know. I have served it at many events with great success. The portobello mushrooms and hominy give it a very satisfying mouthfeel. You can, of course, adjust the heat and serve additional hot sauce on the side. This can be served as is or with rice.

YIELD | 12 TO 16 SERVINGS

3	tablespoons olive oil
2	yellow onions, diced
2	tablespoons minced garlic
1½	pounds portobello mushroom caps (about 5 large), cut into 1½-inch cubes
1	large red bell pepper, scorched, skinned, and diced (see page 10)
2	zucchini, scraped, halved lengthwise, and sliced
3	tablespoons chili powder
1	tablespoon ground cumin
2	teaspoons ground cinnamon
2	teaspoons ground allspice
3	tablespoons fresh oregano leaves or 1 tablespoon dried
1	tablespoon salt

½	teaspoon ground Aleppo chili pepper or ⅛ teaspoon cayenne pepper, or to taste
1	package (12–14 ounces) frozen cut corn kernels
2	cans (15.5 ounces each) black beans, rinsed and drained
1	can (20 ounces) hominy
2	cans (28 ounces each) diced tomatoes
¼	cup chopped fresh cilantro, for garnish
24	ounces (3 cups) sour cream, for serving
2	cups shredded cheddar or Jack cheese, for serving
1	cup pickled jalapeño chili pepper slices, for serving

Heat the oil in a heavy saucepan or cast-iron skillet over medium-high heat. Add the onions and garlic and cook, stirring, until golden, about 5 minutes. Add the mushrooms and bell pepper, lower the heat, and cook, stirring, for 10 minutes. Remove the onions, garlic, and mushrooms from the pan and set aside. Add the zucchini to the pan, adding more oil if necessary, and cook, stirring, until lightly browned, about 5 minutes.

In a 6-quart Dutch oven or slow cooker, stir together the reserved onions, garlic, and mushrooms, and the bell pepper, zucchini, chili powder, cumin, cinnamon, allspice, oregano, salt, and Aleppo or cayenne pepper. Stir in the corn and beans. Rinse the hominy and use your hands to separate the kernels, then add to the pot along with the tomatoes. Stir well. Cover the Dutch oven and cook over medium-low heat for 3 hours, stirring occasionally. If using a slow cooker, set the heat to low and cook for 6 to 8 hours, or follow the manufacturer's directions.

If not serving immediately, let cool, cover, and refrigerate for up to 24 hours. Heat over medium-low heat for 15 to 20 minutes, or until hot, in your kitchen or at your destination. If transporting, carry in a thermal container.

To serve the dish: Serve directly from the cooking pot, garnished with the cilantro. Set out bowls of the sour cream, cheese, and chili peppers.

POTLUCK NOTE | *Ground aleppo chili is a mild, aromatic Middle Eastern spice.*

GAZPACHO WITH GARLIC CROUTONS

For hundreds of years, some form of this cold salad-and-bread soup has been eaten in southern Spain. The tomatoes are a New World addition. If you can get it, try using Spanish extra-virgin olive oil. In the Mediterranean, olives are as diverse as apples are in the United States; as a result, the oils vary. Gazpacho is thought of as a summer food, but it makes a great potluck luncheon dish instead of the usual salad.

YIELD | 3 QUARTS (10 ONE-CUP SERVINGS)

1	tablespoon sugar	1	green bell pepper, peeled, seeded, and diced (see page 105 for peeling instructions)
½	cup + 3 tablespoons Spanish (or other) extra-virgin olive oil	1	large Spanish onion, diced
4	slices French bread (crusts removed), torn into pieces	1	cup minced homemade or store-bought oil-packed sun-dried tomatoes
2	cloves garlic, peeled and sliced	6	cups tomato juice
10	large ripe tomatoes, peeled, seeded, and chopped	3	tablespoons dry sherry or wine vinegar
2	jalapeño chili peppers, halved, seeded, and minced (optional or to taste)	½	cup chopped fresh flat-leaf parsley, for garnish
3	cucumbers, peeled, seeded, and diced	½	cup chopped fresh cilantro, for garnish
1	red bell pepper, peeled, seeded, and diced (see page 105 for peeling instructions)		Garlic Croutons (recipe follows), for garnish

In a large bowl, stir together all the ingredients except the parsley, cilantro, and croutons. In batches, transfer to a covered blender or food processor and pulse for a few seconds until coarsely blended. Do not puree; this soup tastes best when bits of vegetables are still visible. Return to the bowl, cover, and refrigerate for at least 2 hours before serving or for 1 day.

To serve the dish: Remove from the refrigerator, stir, let rest for 15 minutes, and garnish with the parsley, cilantro, and Garlic Croutons. A nice accompaniment for this cold soup might be bowls of assorted olives and roasted almonds.

(continued)

Garlic Croutons

3	slices whole wheat bread	3	cloves garlic, minced
⅓	cup Spanish or other extra-virgin olive oil	½	teaspoon garlic powder

Preheat the oven to 400°F.

Remove the crust from the bread and cut into ½-inch cubes.

Mix the oil, garlic, and garlic powder in a bowl. Stir the bread in the oil mixture so that all sides are coated. Place on a baking sheet and bake until browned, about 10 minutes. Let cool on a rack and serve immediately, or store in an airtight container for up to 2 days.

DESSERTS

THESE VERSATILE DESSERTS, COOKIES, AND SWEETS are welcome at any meal as well as at teas, meetings, and open houses.

I've found that everyone likes great puddings of one kind or another. They are a very good dessert choice because portion control is self-determined. Most of these desserts can be made a day before they are to be eaten, removed from the refrigerator, and served with the chill off or at room temperature. The desserts here are complete as they are, but they're traditionally served with a dollop of whipped cream or a small scoop of ice cream. Any variety of sweet or sour cream blends, plain or frozen yogurts, or fresh berries is always welcome.

The cookies I've included are all easy to transport and can be made in advance and stored in the freezer or at room temperature. They're best packed between layers of waxed or parchment paper and carried in flat containers with tight covers. Most cookies can be layered with parchment or waxed paper and stored in an air-tight container for several days or a week. I have eaten 10-day-old biscotti with pleasure, but all baked goods unless otherwise specified are best a day or two after baking.

If you are going to be making lots of cookies, the biggest luxury is to have four 18-by-12-inch baking sheets so that you can put a second batch in the oven without waiting. Also useful are Silpat nonstick silicone baking liners. At 17 by 11 inches, they fit most baking sheets and can be used at temperatures up to approximately 475°F. To make the sweets in this chapter, you should have an 8-by-8-inch baking pan, a 9-by-9-inch baking pan, and a 13-by-9-inch pan that you can use for baking and serving small sweets.

DOUBLE CHOCOLATE PUDDING

The romance of chocolate is heady stuff. From homey puddings to artful confections, rich cakes, and chocolate moles that bite back, few people seem indifferent to its lure. This recipe is as much fun to make as it is to eat because of the chocolatey aroma.

YIELD | 10 SERVINGS

4	large egg yolks, at room temperature	1	cup (8 ounces) heavy cream
¾	cup sugar	2	teaspoons pure vanilla extract
2	cups whole milk	½	cup unsweetened cocoa powder
3	tablespoons cornstarch	4	ounces dark chocolate, melted
⅛	teaspoon salt		

In a bowl, beat the egg yolks and sugar until light.

In a medium saucepan over medium heat, bring 1¾ cups of the milk to the boiling point. Remove from the heat and slowly add the milk to the egg-and-sugar mixture, whisking constantly. Pour the mixture back into the saucepan.

In a measuring cup, whisk the cornstarch with the remaining ¼ cup of milk to form a smooth mixture. Add the cornstarch mixture and salt to the saucepan. Heat, stirring constantly, until thick enough to coat the back of a wooden spoon, 5 to 7 minutes. Add the cream and vanilla, stir, and remove from the heat.

Whisk in the cocoa and chocolate. Stir and pour into a serving bowl. Let cool thoroughly, cover with plastic wrap, and refrigerate until thick and cold, at least 4 hours and up to 24 hours.

To serve the dish: Serve cold with whipped cream, crème fraîche (or 1 cup heavy cream mixed with ¼ cup sour cream), and/or fresh raspberries.

POTLUCK NOTE | *To test the thickness of the pudding on the back of a wooden spoon, run the tip of a teaspoon through the coating. If it leaves a clear strip in the pudding, it's thick enough. To chill the pudding quickly, pour it into a metal mixing bowl, place in a larger bowl of ice water, and stir the pudding for 10 minutes. This ice-water bath is useful in many applications.*

BANANA PUDDING WITH MERINGUE

I thought my taste was way too sophisticated to even try banana pudding. When I was in Savannah, Georgia, interviewing Paula Deen before she became a household name, she suggested that I try her banana pudding. What had I been thinking? This is my potluck version. Thanks, Paula!

YIELD | 10 TO 12 SERVINGS

1½	cups vanilla wafer crumbs	¼	teaspoon salt
4	tablespoons (¼ cup) unsalted butter, melted	3	very ripe bananas, mashed but not pureed
2	cups whole milk	2	teaspoons pure vanilla extract
4	eggs, separated	3	ripe, firm bananas, sliced
¾	cup sugar	4–5	dozen vanilla wafers
¼	cup instant flour		Meringue (recipe follows)

Preheat the oven to 350°F.

In a small bowl, mix the wafer crumbs and butter, spread and press on the bottom of an 18-by-9-inch baking pan.

In a medium bowl, whisk together the milk and egg yolks.

In the top of a double boiler over simmering water, stir together the sugar, flour, and salt. Whisk in the egg-yolk mixture. Continue whisking to blend well and cook until the mixture thickens, 10 to 15 minutes. Stir occasionally to incorporate the thicker portion on the bottom of the pan. Remove from the heat and stir in the mashed bananas and vanilla. In the baking pan, alternate layers of the custard mixture, banana slices, and wafers, repeating two or three times.

Spread the Meringue on the pudding, using a spatula to seal the edges.

Bake until golden brown, about 15 minutes.

Meringue

| 4 | egg whites | ⅓ | cup superfine sugar |
| ½ | teaspoon cream of tartar | 1 | teaspoon pure vanilla extract |

Using an electric mixer on low speed, beat the egg whites until frothy. Add the cream of tartar and sugar and beat until stiff, glossy peaks form. Add the vanilla toward the end.

POTLUCK NOTE | *Serve warm or cold. If you want to skip the Meringue, sprinkle the top of the pudding with a cup of vanilla wafer crumbs to finish it and serve with whipped cream or a mixture of heavy cream and sour cream, sprinkled with brown sugar.*

TIRAMISU

Tiramisu, which translates literally as "pick-me-up," is an Italian dessert that traditionally consists of ladyfingers, mascarpone cheese, cocoa, espresso, liquor, eggs, sugar, and cream. Some culinary detectives think that it developed in Tuscany after World War I and was based on the British trifle, while others believe it dates back to the Renaissance. Certainly by the end of the 18th century, sugar, coffee, and cocoa were treats in the Friuli-Venezia region, as was creamy mascarpone cheese. So luscious is this dish that some say it was prepared for Casanova to keep his energy and spirits up. In any event, this dessert, in all its variations, inspires romantic stories.

YIELD | 12 SERVINGS

6	egg yolks	2	cups brewed or instant espresso, cooled
1	cup sugar	40	large ladyfingers or Savoiardi biscuits
⅔	cup marsala, port, or Madeira		
1	pound mascarpone cheese	3	tablespoons unsweetened cocoa powder
2	cups (1 pint) heavy cream whipped with ½ cup sugar		Shaved chocolate for garnish

In the top of a double boiler over simmering water, whisk the egg yolks, sugar, and wine. Stir constantly until the mixture is thick and just before the boiling point, about 4 minutes. Remove from the heat at the sight of any bubbles.

In a large bowl, beat the custard into the cheese until well incorporated. When it is at room temperature, fold in the whipped cream.

Place the coffee in a shallow bowl. Dip the ladyfingers or biscuits briefly into the coffee, then arrange in a single layer in a 12-by-9-inch serving dish. Top with a layer of the mascarpone mixture, then a layer of espresso-soaked ladyfingers or biscuits, and repeat, ending with a mascarpone layer. Smooth with a spatula.

When the cake is assembled, sprinkle with the cocoa from a shaker and chill for several hours. It can also be frozen very successfully and brought to refrigerator or room temperature before serving. Garnish with shaved chocolate before serving the tiramisu.

POTLUCK NOTE | *If you can't find ladyfingers or Savoiardi biscuits, you can use pound cake. Cut it into ¾-inch slices, then cut each slice into three strips.*

DOUBLE-RICH BUTTERSCOTCH PUDDING

I like this pudding so much that I once took a sample of it to one of my favorite restaurants and begged them to put it on the menu.

YIELD | 12 SERVINGS

9	tablespoons unsalted butter, cut into slices	3	cups whole milk
2½	cups packed dark brown sugar	6	large egg yolks
2	cups (1 pint) heavy cream	6	tablespoons cornstarch
		½	teaspoon salt

Melt the butter in a heavy saucepan over medium heat. Gradually stir in the sugar until incorporated. Cook until the mixture is smooth and simmering, stirring occasionally, about 5 minutes.

Meanwhile, heat the cream over low heat until warm.

Lower the heat under the sugar and gradually add the cream. Cook, stirring, until blended, about 2 minutes. Remove the pan from the heat.

In the top of a large double boiler, whisk the milk, egg yolks, cornstarch, and salt. Place over simmering water over medium heat, and gradually stir in the sugar-and-cream mixture. Stir or gently whisk constantly until the pudding thickens, about 12 minutes. Reduce the heat to low, cover, and cook another 10 minutes, stirring occasionally.

Remove from the heat and let cool for 10 minutes, still stirring occasionally. Pour into twelve 1-cup serving dishes or a 3-quart serving bowl. Chill thoroughly before serving.

The pudding can be refrigerated covered for 2 days before serving. Do not cover the pudding until it is cold, or steam will form.

To serve the dish: Serve cold, as is, or with dollops of whipped cream and/or toasted, finely sliced almonds.

S'MORES BREAD PUDDING

This dish, based on a childhood favorite, is really a meal in itself. I recommend it when the main course is a salad or other fish dish. Any leftovers can be frozen, brought to room temperature, and warmed in a preheated oven. But it won't be the same.

YIELD | 15 SERVINGS

12	ounces dark chocolate, chopped	1	cup milk
8	tablespoons (½ cup) unsalted butter, sliced	1	jar (16 ounces) marshmallow cream
2	pounds challah or baguettes, cut into 2-inch cubes	40	individual graham crackers, coarsely broken, divided
2	cups half-and-half	20	large marshmallows, halved horizontally
8	large eggs		
⅔	cup sugar	⅔	cup chocolate chips

Preheat the oven to 350°F. Lightly butter a 13-by-9-inch oven-to-table baking dish.

Melt the dark chocolate and butter in the top of a double boiler so that the bottom doesn't touch the water simmering in the lower half, then let it come to room temperature. In a large bowl, soak the bread in the half-and-half for 20 minutes for challah, 30 minutes for baguettes. In a large bowl, whisk together the eggs, sugar, and milk. Whisk in the chocolate-and-butter mixture and blend well, then pour over the soaked bread and mix thoroughly.

In a medium bowl, lightly mix the marshmallow cream with half of the graham crackers. (This will be messy and a good time to assist the rubber spatula with a gloved hand.)

Place half of the bread mixture in the prepared baking dish, spreading it out from edge to edge. Layer the marshmallow-cream mixture on top. Cover first with the remaining bread mixture, then with the remaining graham crackers. Top with the marshmallow halves and sprinkle with the chocolate chips.

Bake until firm, about 35 minutes. Remove from the oven and allow to cool. This pudding is best made and served without holding in the refrigerator.

To serve the dish: Serve at room temperature as is, or accompanied by whipped cream or vanilla ice cream.

POACHED PEARS WITH WHITE WINE AND SHAVED PARMESAN CHEESE

I have had varieties of this dish in Italy, where fruit and cheese are combined in endless ways for a very refreshing end to a meal. The saffron is optional, but it has a lovely flavor.

YIELD | 10 SERVINGS

10	firm, ripe pears	2	tablespoons fresh lemon juice
1	large bowl of water with the juice of 1 lemon	2	teaspoons ground cinnamon
2	cups water	1	wedge (12 ounces) Parmesan cheese
2	cups white wine		Fresh basil leaves, for garnish (optional)
	Large pinch of saffron (optional)		
½	cup honey, mild if you are using saffron, strong if not		

Peel the pears, leaving the stems intact if possible, and core them from the bottom with a melon baller. Place in the lemon water so they do not discolor.

In a large pot, combine the 2 cups water, wine, saffron (if using), honey, lemon juice, and cinnamon. Place over high heat, bring to a low boil, and reduce the heat to medium.

Using a slotted spoon, remove the pears from the lemon water and add them to the poaching liquid. Simmer until fork-tender, about 35 minutes. Remove the pears with a slotted spoon, let cool, then refrigerate until cold.

Cook the poaching liquid until reduced by half, 30 to 45 minutes. Remove from the heat, let cool, then refrigerate until cold.

To serve the dish: Set the pears upright in a deep platter, douse with the poaching syrup, and surround with shavings of the cheese. Garnish with the basil, if using.

POTLUCK NOTE | *If preparing whole pears is too fussy for you, simply peel them, cut in half from top to bottom, core, and poach for 20 minutes. You can also eliminate the cheese and serve with a thick chocolate-fudge sauce.*

SUMMER PUDDING

This pudding couldn't be easier to make. Use any combination of ripe berries and, if you can find them, fresh currants. I've made this with conventional store-bought white, oatmeal, wheat, and raisin bread with equal success. It's most attractive made in a charlotte mold, but a 3-quart pudding mold or mixing bowl will do just as well.

YIELD | 12 SERVINGS

3	tablespoons unsalted butter, softened	½	pound (1 pint) blackberries, rinsed and halved
1	pound (1½ pints) strawberries, rinsed, hulled, and quartered	1	cup sugar, or to taste
1	pound (1½ pints) raspberries, rinsed	1	loaf sliced white bread, crusts removed
½	pound cherries, rinsed, pitted, and halved		

Grease a charlotte mold or 3-quart mixing bowl with 1 tablespoon of the butter. Line the bowl with plastic wrap, leaving extra to cover the pudding. Use about 1½ tablespoons of the butter to grease the plastic wrap.

In a large bowl, mix the fruit and dredge with the sugar. Taste and add a bit more sugar if you like, but keep in mind that too much will overpower the fruit.

Line the charlotte mold with the bread, overlapping where necessary. Start at the bottom and work up to ½ inch from the top of the bowl. Using a cup, add a layer of fruit. Cover the fruit with another layer of bread, pressing gently. Repeat until all the fruit is used. Finish with a layer of bread. Spread the remaining ½ tablespoon butter over all and cover with plastic wrap. Place a plate directly on top of the plastic so that it rests on the pudding, and weigh the plate down with cans from the cupboard. If you don't have a plate that fits, cut a piece of cardboard. Refrigerate for 8 hours or overnight.

To serve the dish: To unmold the pudding, remove the top plate and weights, and unfold the plastic. Place a flat platter that is larger than the rim of the bowl over the top and turn it upside down. Holding one hand on the open plastic wrap, gently loosen it all around the bowl onto the plate. Gently lift the bowl and you will have a perfect dome. Peel away the plastic wrap. Serve with whipped cream or custard sauce.

ROASTED SUMMER STONE FRUIT WITH RICOTTA

Roasting fruit brings out its essence and sugar. This dish is the perfect light ending to any meal. It is very satisfying served cold either on its own or with a dollop of yogurt mixed with honey. You'll find your own combinations and accompaniments.

YIELD | 10 SERVINGS

1	pound firm, ripe red plums, washed, pitted, and halved (2 cups)
1	pound firm, ripe peaches, washed, pitted, and quartered (2 cups)
1	pound firm, ripe apricots, washed, pitted, and halved (2 cups)
1	pound firm, ripe nectarines, washed, pitted, and quartered (2 cups)

½	cup granulated sugar
3	cups whole-milk or low-fat ricotta cheese
½	cup superfine sugar
2	tablespoons fresh Meyer lemon or mandarin orange juice
2	teaspoons Meyer lemon or mandarin orange zest (see page 262)

Preheat the oven to 400°F. Spray or brush a jelly-roll pan with oil.

Lay the fruit skin side down on the prepared pan and sprinkle with the granulated sugar. Roast until the edges of the fruit look brown and caramelized, about 20 minutes. Don't overcook, or the fruit will lose its shape. Remove from the oven and let cool.

In a medium bowl, using a flat whisk or large fork, mix the ricotta cheese, superfine sugar, lemon or orange juice, and lemon or orange zest. This mixture can be covered and refrigerated until ready to serve or carry to your destination.

To serve the dish: Arrange the fruit on a platter and intersperse with dollops of the ricotta mixture. The fruit is best served the same day, warm or at room temperature.

BAKED APPLES WITH BALSAMIC REDUCTION

Baked apples do not seem as popular as they once were, but I think you'll find that most people like them—I know I do. The balsamic reduction is a modern touch.

YIELD | 10 SERVINGS

1½	cups balsamic vinegar	1	teaspoon ground cinnamon
5	tablespoons + ⅔ cup firmly packed brown sugar	½	teaspoon ground nutmeg
10	medium/large red cooking apples	2	cups apple juice or water
½	cup currants, raisins, or dried cherries		

Preheat the oven to 375°F.

Place the vinegar and 5 tablespoons brown sugar in a small heavy-bottomed saucepan over medium-low heat and bring to the boiling point. Lower the heat and simmer—do not let it boil—until the liquid is reduced by half, 20 to 30 minutes. Remove from the heat.

Wash and core the apples with a corer or melon baller, leaving at least ½ inch on the bottoms. Remove a 1-inch strip of peel around the top of each apple and stand the apples upright in one or two 13-by-10-inch baking dish(es).

In a small bowl, mix the dried fruit, cinnamon, nutmeg, and the remaining ⅔ cup brown sugar. Spoon equal amounts into the center of each apple.

Add the apple juice or water to the baking dish to cover the bottom. Drizzle the tops of the apples with the balsamic reduction and bake until the apples are fork-tender, 30 to 40 minutes.

To serve the dish: Some people like this dish warm; others, cold—your choice. Carefully place the apples upright on a large platter with the syrup from the baking pan. If you prefer, you can plate them individually in deep dessert dishes with a little of the pan syrup over each apple.

BLUEBERRY GRUNT

A grunt, which is basically a fruit stew with dumplings, is so named because of the sound the boiling fruit makes as it pops air bubbles in the dough. It is a Southern specialty, and in a Daufuskie Island, South Carolina, cookbook, the instructions are to boil the berries, drop in the "doe," and cook on the back of a wood stove until done. And then, "Eat 'em hot er cold."

YIELD | 10 SERVINGS

Filling

1	cup water	1	tablespoon fresh lemon juice
1	cup turbinado or packed light brown sugar	1	teaspoon finely grated lemon zest (see page 262)
½	teaspoon cinnamon	3	pints (5 cups) fresh blueberries, rinsed
½	teaspoon ground nutmeg		

Topping

2	cups all-purpose flour	5	tablespoons unsalted butter, sliced and softened
1	tablespoon baking powder	¾	cup milk
½	teaspoon salt		
1	tablespoon + 1 teaspoon granulated sugar		

To make the filling: In a 3-quart cast-iron Dutch oven or any wide, heavy 3-quart pot with a lid, bring the water, brown sugar, cinnamon, nutmeg, lemon juice, and lemon zest to the boiling point over medium heat. Stir in the blueberries and return to the boiling point. Lower the heat and simmer, uncovered, stirring frequently, until the berries are somewhat crushed but still hold their shape, about 15 minutes.

To make the topping: In a medium bowl, blend together the flour, baking powder, salt, and granulated sugar. With a pastry blender or two butter knives, cut in the butter until the mixture resembles coarse crumbs. Add the milk and stir slightly with a fork, leaving the batter lumpy. To avoid hot splashes, remove the pot of berries from the heat and drop dough by the spoonful over the berries. Place the lid on the pot and cook over medium heat for 15 minutes. Don't peek during cooking or the dough will deflate. Let cool for 20 minutes before serving.

To serve the dish: At a buffet, use a deep serving spoon to serve from the pot it was cooked in. You can also plate it into individual dessert bowls.

DRIED WINTER FRUIT COMPOTE
WITH RAISIN SAUCE

This is another one of those dishes that you can make your own by choosing whatever dried fruit, liquor, and/or spice you prefer. Star anise and sliced lemon can be added, and honey can replace the sugar.

YIELD | 10 SERVINGS

1	pound dried figs, preferably whole, not pressed
½	pound dried plums, pitted and picked over for broken pits
½	pound dried pears
½	pound dried apple slices
½	pound dried mango or papaya
¼	pound dried blueberries
¼	pound dried cherries, pitted and picked over for broken pits

3	quarts boiling water
¾	cup bourbon or any golden brown liquor such as brandy or scotch, or an equal amount of water
½	cup sugar
2	teaspoons ground cinnamon
	Raisin Sauce (recipe follows)

Place all the fruit in a large heatproof bowl and mix together. Pour the boiling water over the fruit. Let rest for 45 minutes, stirring two or three times. Drain the fruit and set aside 1½ cups of the liquid.

In a saucepan large enough to hold all the ingredients, heat the liquor, reserved liquid, sugar, and cinnamon to the boiling point over medium-low heat. Add the drained fruit, lower the heat, and simmer gently for 30 minutes.

Let cool, remove to a serving bowl, cover, and chill for up to 24 hours before serving. This can keep longer, but the fruit will get softer.

To serve the dish: Place the fruit in a deep serving dish with a ladle, and accompany with the Raisin Sauce in a smaller bowl with a small ladle.

(continued)

Raisin Sauce

1	cup raisins, soaked in 1½ cups water for 24 hours, then drained	1	cup (8 ounces) heavy cream
2	cups light sour cream	½	teaspoon pure vanilla extract
		⅓	cup pure maple syrup

In a large bowl, mix all the ingredients, cover, and refrigerate for up to 24 hours.

POTLUCK NOTE | *For a dramatic presentation, make sure the compote is in a heatproof dish. Place ¼ cup bourbon in a long-handled soup ladle. Hold it at arm's length and light it with a long match. Tilt the flaming liquor into the compote. Wait until the flame goes out before inserting the serving spoon.*

CRUNCHY APPLE CRISP

In the fall, when markets have an abundance of apples, this is the dish to make. Mixing a variety of apples enriches the flavor. Pears can be substituted or mixed half-and-half with the apples. If you have them on hand, toss in a cup of frozen or dried cranberries.

YIELD | 10 SERVINGS

Filling

6	cups sliced assorted apples, such as Rome, McIntosh, and Granny Smith	1	teaspoon ground cinnamon
		½	teaspoon ground cardamom
¼	cup granulated sugar	¼	teaspoon ground cloves
1	tablespoon fresh lemon juice		

Topping

1	cup all-purpose flour	1	teaspoon ground cinnamon
1	cup rolled oats	10	tablespoons unsalted butter, sliced
1	cup packed brown or granulated sugar	½	cup chopped walnuts

Preheat the oven to 375°F. Lightly butter a 10-by-13-inch baking dish.

To make the filling: In a large bowl, toss the apples with the sugar, lemon juice, cinnamon, cardamom, and cloves. Layer on the bottom of the prepared baking dish.

To make the topping: In a medium mixing bowl, stir together the flour, oats, sugar, and cinnamon. With a pastry blender or two butter knives, cut in the butter until it resembles coarse crumbs. Do not overmix. With your hands, sprinkle the topping over the apples, then sprinkle the walnuts on top of that.

Bake until the apples are fork-tender, about 30 minutes.

To serve the dish: Serve hot from the oven or at room temperature. Cinnamon ice cream or low-fat vanilla yogurt mixed with cinnamon are great accompaniments.

GINGER-PEACHY COBBLER

There are as many cobbler recipes as there are states in the Union. In summer you can make cobblers with almost any stone fruit, and in winter you can use apples and pears. It's best to sauté winter fruit in some butter and sugar or maple syrup before putting it in the baking pan.

YIELD | 10 SERVINGS

Filling

6	cups sliced ripe peaches (about 8)	½	teaspoon ground nutmeg
⅓	cup packed brown sugar	⅓	cup minced candied ginger
½	teaspoon ground ginger	1	tablespoon fresh lemon juice

Topping

10	tablespoons cold unsalted butter, sliced	1	cup granulated sugar
2¼	cups self-rising flour	1	cup buttermilk or whole milk
⅛	teaspoon salt		

Preheat the oven to 375°F. Lightly butter a 13-by-9-inch baking dish.

To make the filling: In a large bowl, toss together the peaches, sugar, ground ginger, nutmeg, and candied ginger. Spoon into the prepared baking dish and drizzle the lemon juice over all.

To make the topping: In a large bowl, using a pastry blender or two butter knives, incorporate the butter, flour, and salt until the mixture resembles coarse crumbs. Stir in the sugar and milk only until incorporated. Drop by spoonfuls on top of the peach mixture.

Bake until the fruit is bubbling and the topping is golden brown, about 35 minutes. Cool at least 30 minutes, up to 3 hours, at room temperature.

To serve the dish: Serve warm or cold. Accompany with a pitcher of cold heavy cream, yogurt mixed with honey, or vanilla ice cream.

CHERRY CLAFOUTI

This is a traditional French "made at home" dish that is best served within an hour or two after it is made. Chilling toughens it a bit, so it is recommended that you make it just before leaving the house if you are taking it to an event. Think of it as a terrific last-minute dessert. If the oven will be free at your destination, consider bringing a baking pan and the ingredients in three plastic containers: one with the pitted cherries, with or without kirsch; another with the flour and sugar; and the third with the remaining ingredients.

YIELD | 10 SERVINGS

3½	cups sweet cherries, pitted	1	large egg yolk
¼	cup kirsch (optional)	1	cup milk
¾	cup instant flour	1	cup heavy cream
½	cup granulated sugar	2	teaspoons pure vanilla extract
4	large eggs		Confectioners' sugar, for dusting

Preheat the oven to 375°F. Lightly butter a 13-by-9-inch baking dish.

If using kirsch, place the cherries in a bowl, pour on the liqueur, and let soak for 15 minutes. Drain the cherries, then spread them in the prepared baking dish.

In a small bowl, mix the flour and sugar. In a large bowl, whisk the eggs and egg yolk, then whisk in the milk and cream. Beat in the flour mixture. Add the vanilla, stir, and pour the topping evenly over the cherries.

Bake until slightly puffed and browned, about 35 minutes. Let cool for 10 to 15 minutes before serving.

To serve the dish: Serve warm or cool, dusted with confectioners' sugar.

TRIPLE-CHOCOLATE COOKIES

These need no introduction; they are a chocoholic's dream come true.

YIELD | 36 TO 42 COOKIES

1½	teaspoons baking soda
2¼	cups flour
1	cup (½ pound) unsalted butter
½	cup granulated sugar
½	cup brown sugar
2	eggs, lightly beaten
1	teaspoon pure vanilla extract
6	ounces milk chocolate, coarsely chopped
6	ounces white chocolate, coarsely chopped
6	ounces dark chocolate, coarsely chopped

Preheat the oven to 375°F. Set out two baking sheets, unbuttered or lined with Silpat liners.

In a medium bowl, stir the baking soda into the flour.

In a large bowl, using an electric mixer, cream the butter and the sugars. Beat in the eggs and vanilla. Stir in the flour mixture, then stir in all the chocolate.

Drop the batter by heaping tablespoons 2 inches apart on the baking sheets. Bake until the edges darken slightly, 10 to 12 minutes.

Remove the cookies with a spatula to cake racks to cool completely. Eat within 24 hours.

POTLUCK NOTE | *Unless you think you are going to need all of the cookies, reserve a few from each batch and wrap them in plastic, then in foil. Label them clearly, being sure to include the date, and freeze. (Encircle anything you are freezing with masking tape—labeled with a waterproof marker—so it doesn't fall off and leave you with mystery packages.) In time you will have a terrific assortment of cookies that can be thawed and served at a spontaneous event.*

VERY CHOCOLATE BROWNIES

YIELD | 16 BROWNIES

⅔	cup all-purpose flour + more for dusting	8	ounces semisweet chocolate, chopped, or chocolate chips
¼	cup instant flour	3	large eggs
½	teaspoon baking soda	¾	cup sugar
¼	teaspoon salt	1½	teaspoons pure vanilla extract
6	tablespoons unsalted butter, sliced + more for greasing	¾	cup chopped walnuts (optional)

Preheat the oven to 325°F. Lightly butter and dust with flour a 9-by-9-inch baking pan.

In a small bowl, sift or stir together the ⅔ cup all-purpose flour, instant flour, baking soda, and salt.

Melt the 6 tablespoons butter and chocolate in the top of a double boiler set over simmering water. Remove from the heat.

In a large bowl, using an electric mixer, beat the eggs, sugar, and vanilla at medium speed. Add the chocolate mixture and continue beating for 1 minute. Add the flour mixture and beat on low for no more than 30 seconds. If using walnuts, mix them in with a spatula. Pour the batter into the prepared pan and spread evenly with a spatula.

Bake until a cake tester comes out clean, about 40 minutes. Cool in the pan on a rack and cut into squares.

The brownies are best served within a few hours but can remain in the pan, covered with plastic wrap, for up to 24 hours. Don't let the plastic rest on top of the brownies.

Apricot Squares (opposite)
Lemon Squares (page 198)
Raspberry Bars (page 199)

APRICOT SQUARES

Dessert bars and squares are welcome at any gathering. If you want to turn them into bite-size pieces, cut them into squares about 1½ by 1½ inches. Use a very sharp knife so they don't crumble.

YIELD | 16 SQUARES

Crust

½	cup granulated sugar	1½	cups all-purpose flour + more for dusting	
2	egg yolks			
8	tablespoons (½ cup) unsalted butter, cut into slices	¼	teaspoon salt	
		1	teaspoon pure vanilla extract	

Topping

2	eggs, lightly beaten	½	pound dried apricots, plumped in simmering water for 3 minutes, then drained and minced	
⅔	cup turbinado or packed light brown sugar			
		1	cup apricot or apple jelly, melted	

Preheat the oven to 350°F. Butter and lightly flour an 8-by-8-inch baking pan.

To make the crust: In a large bowl, combine the granulated sugar and egg yolks and whisk until light. Add the butter and beat with an electric mixer until smooth. Blend in the 1½ cups flour, salt, and vanilla just until combined. Spread the batter evenly in the prepared pan.

Bake until golden, about 15 minutes. Remove from the oven and let cool for 10 minutes. Maintain the oven temperature.

To make the topping: In a medium bowl, stir together the eggs, turbinado sugar, and apricots. Spread over the crust. Drizzle the jelly over all. Return to the oven and bake until lightly browned, about 20 minutes.

Let cool completely and cut into sixteen 2-inch squares.

These are best served within a few hours but can remain in the pan, covered with plastic wrap, for up to 24 hours. Don't let the plastic rest on top of the Apricot Squares.

LEMON SQUARES

Crust

8	tablespoons (½ cup) unsalted butter, chilled and cut into pieces + more for greasing	⅓	cup packed light brown sugar
		1¼	cups all-purpose flour
		¼	teaspoon salt

Topping

1	cup granulated sugar	2	tablespoons unsalted butter, melted
2	large eggs		
½	cup fresh lemon juice (from 2–3 lemons)	3	tablespoons instant flour
			Confectioners' sugar, for dusting
1	tablespoon lemon zest (see page 262)		

Preheat the oven to 350°F. Lightly butter an 8-by-8-inch baking pan.

To make the crust: In a large bowl, using an electric mixer, cream the 8 tablespoons butter and brown sugar until light and fluffy. Add the all-purpose flour and salt and beat until just blended. Do not overmix.

Press the dough into the bottom of the prepared pan and bake until browned, about 15 minutes. Remove from the oven and let cool on a cake rack. Maintain the oven temperature.

To make the topping: In a medium bowl, using an electric mixer, beat the granulated sugar and eggs until light. Add the lemon juice and lemon zest and stir to combine. Stir in the butter and incorporate the instant flour until it disappears. Pour over the crust and smooth it from edge to edge with a spatula.

Bake until set, 20 to 25 minutes.

Let cool on a cake rack. Cut into sixteen 2-inch squares and dust with confectioners' sugar when completely cool.

Lemon Squares are best served within a few hours but can remain in the pan, covered with plastic wrap, for up to 24 hours. Don't let the plastic rest on top of the squares.

RASPBERRY BARS

YIELD | 18 BARS

Filling

2½	cups (1½ pints) raspberries, rinsed	1	tablespoon fresh lemon juice
2	tablespoons granulated sugar	1	tablespoon instant tapioca
2	tablespoons water	½	teaspoon ground cinnamon

Crust

1	cup all-purpose flour	¾	cup packed brown sugar
1	teaspoon baking soda	½	teaspoon ground cinnamon
¼	teaspoon salt	8	tablespoons (½ cup) unsalted butter, melted
1	cup quick-cooking oats (not instant)		

Preheat the oven to 350°F.

To make the filling: In a medium saucepan, combine all the filling ingredients. Bring just to the boiling point over medium heat, then reduce the heat and simmer, stirring frequently, for 5 minutes, or until slightly thickened. Remove from the heat.

To make the crust: In a large mixing bowl, stir together the flour, baking soda, salt, oats, brown sugar, and cinnamon. Stir in the butter until incorporated. Set aside 1 cup for topping. With your fingertips, press the remaining flour mixture into an ungreased 9-by-9-inch baking pan.

Bake the crust until pale brown, about 20 minutes. Remove from the oven but maintain the oven temperature. Using a rubber spatula, gently spread the filling over the hot crust. Sprinkle the reserved flour mixture over the filling. Lightly press the topping with the back of a spoon.

Bake until the filling is set, another 20 to 25 minutes. Let cool in the pan on a cake rack, then cut into 3-by-1½-inch bars.

These are best served within a few hours but can remain in the pan, covered with plastic wrap, for up to 24 hours. Don't let the plastic rest on top of the bars.

NEW YORK BLACK-AND-WHITE COOKIES

These cookies are available at just about every New York deli and diner. They have started making inroads in the other 49 states as well, but nothing beats the fresh-baked taste of these.

YIELD | 24 LARGE COOKIES

2½	cups all-purpose flour
2½	cups cake flour
1	teaspoon baking powder
½	teaspoon salt
8	tablespoons (½ cup) unsalted butter, sliced and softened + more for greasing

1¾	cups sugar
4	eggs, lightly beaten
1	cup milk
½	teaspoon pure vanilla extract
¼	teaspoon pure lemon extract
	Black and White Icings (recipe follows)

Preheat the oven to 375°F. Butter two baking sheets for the first batch or use Silpat sheets. They will be cooled, rebuttered, and used again.

In a medium bowl, using a fork, mix together the flours, baking powder, and salt.

In a large bowl, using an electric mixer, cream the 8 tablespoons butter, then gradually cream in the sugar until the mixture is light and fluffy. Beat in the eggs, milk, and vanilla and lemon extracts. Add 2 cups of the flour mixture and beat. Remove the beaters and stir in the remaining flour mixture until thoroughly incorporated. Do not overmix. Using a 2-tablespoon measure, such as an ice cream scoop, drop the batter 2 inches apart on the prepared baking sheets, about six cookies per sheet.

Bake in the top and bottom thirds of the oven until the cookie edges start to brown, about 20 minutes. If you think that your oven is unevenly heated—and most are—halfway through baking, reverse the cookie sheets from the top and bottom shelves and turn them around front to back, then continue baking.

Remove the baking sheets but maintain the oven heat. Using a spatula, transfer the cookies to a cake rack and let cool completely.

(continued)

Let the baking sheets come to room temperature, then butter and repeat, measuring 2 tablespoons of batter to make another 12 cookies on two sheets. Bake as before.

Make the icings.

When the cookies are cool, set them flat side up on waxed paper. Using a small offset spatula, spread white icing on half of each cookie. Then use a clean spatula to coat the other half of the cookie with chocolate icing. Let set.

These are best served within 24 hours but can be layered with waxed paper and refrigerate for 2 to 3 days.

Black and White Icings

3½	cups confectioners' sugar	⅓	cup unsweetened Dutch-process cocoa powder
3	tablespoons light corn syrup	1½	ounces semisweet chocolate, melted
2	teaspoons fresh lemon juice		
1	teaspoon pure vanilla extract		
4–6	tablespoons water		

In a medium bowl, stir together the sugar, corn syrup, lemon juice, vanilla, and 1 tablespoon of the water until smooth.

Place half of the icing in another bowl. Stir in the cocoa and chocolate. Add more water as needed for a glossy icing.

COCONUT JUMBLES

A jumble is simply a ring-shaped cookie. These easy cookies have an elusive, old-time taste.

YIELD | 30 TO 36 COOKIES

2	cups all-purpose flour	1	cup granulated sugar
½	teaspoon baking soda	2	large eggs, slightly beaten
¼	teaspoon salt	¼	cup sour cream
8	tablespoons (½ cup) unsalted butter + more for greasing	1⅓	cups sweetened coconut Confectioners' sugar, for dusting

Preheat the oven to 375°F. Butter two baking sheets.

In a small bowl, mix together the flour, baking soda, and salt.

In a large bowl, using an electric mixer, cream the 8 tablespoons butter until light and fluffy. Gradually beat in the sugar, then the eggs. Add the sour cream and coconut. Incorporate the flour mixture. Chill the dough for 30 minutes.

Take the dough by heaping tablespoons and roll each into a 5-inch rope. Shape into a ring and pinch the ends together. Place the rings on the baking sheets so that they do not touch.

Bake until golden brown, about 12 minutes. Remove from the oven and let cool for 5 minutes. Remove the jumbles to a cake rack, cool completely, and dust with confectioners' sugar. Store in an airtight container for up to 3 days.

PINE NUT COOKIES

I love these cookies—the pine nuts remind me of the "Indian" nuts in the shell that we ate as kids.

YIELD | 24 COOKIES

2	large egg whites
	Pinch of salt
½	cup confectioners' sugar
8	ounces almond paste, broken into bits
½	cup granulated sugar
¾	cup pine nuts (pignoli)

Preheat the oven to 300°F. Butter and lightly flour two baking sheets or line with Silpat sheets.

In a large bowl, using an electric mixer, beat the egg whites with the salt until quite foamy but not dry. Whisk in the confectioners' sugar, then incorporate the almond paste and granulated sugar until smooth.

Place the pine nuts in a shallow bowl. Keeping hands moist, take a scant tablespoonful of batter at a time and press the top into the pine nuts, making sure the nuts adhere. Drop 2 inches apart on the prepared baking sheets.

Bake until golden brown, 15 to 20 minutes. Cool thoroughly on racks, store in an airtight container, and eat within 24 hours.

HAZELNUT BISCOTTI WITH CHOCOLATE ICING

After living in Italy for a year, I became addicted to unfrosted biscotti with my morning latte—not an Italian custom but a very satisfying one. They are so dense and have no fat, and I am pleased to say that I came back the same size 6. The name "biscotti" translates as "twice" ("bis") "cooked" ("cotti"), which they are. They're delicious and well worth your time because they have a very long shelf life. For a special treat, these do well with chocolate icing. But what doesn't?

YIELD | ABOUT 36 BISCOTTI

1	cup hazelnuts		Pinch of salt
2	cups all-purpose flour	3	large eggs
⅓	cup unsweetened good-quality cocoa powder	1½	cups sugar
1	teaspoon ground cinnamon	¼	pound bittersweet chocolate
1	teaspoon baking powder	2	tablespoons unsalted butter
½	teaspoon baking soda	2	tablespoon chocolate liqueur, such as Godiva or Van Gogh

Preheat the oven to 350°F. Line two 18-by-13-inch baking sheets with parchment paper.

To remove the bitter brown skins from the hazelnuts, spread the nuts in a single layer on a rimmed, unlined baking sheet and toast in the oven for 7 to 9 minutes. Slide onto a clean tea towel. Fold the towel over them and, using your hands, rub them vigorously between the folds. Don't worry if some small bits don't come off.

Coarsely crush or chop the nuts and set aside.

In a medium bowl, stir together the flour, cocoa, cinnamon, baking powder, baking soda, and salt.

In a bowl large enough to hold all the ingredients, whisk the eggs and sugar. Stir in the dry ingredients, then the reserved hazelnuts. The dough will be quite thick and sticky.

Using your hands, divide the dough into two flat logs, each about 3½ inches wide and 10 inches long. Place both on one prepared baking sheet and bake until they are

(continued)

slightly browned and a toothpick comes out clean, 20 to 25 minutes. Remove from the oven and reduce the oven temperature to 300°F. Transfer the logs to a cutting surface. While they are still warm, cut into ½-inch slices.

Reline the used baking sheet with fresh parchment. Place the biscotti cut side down on the prepared sheets and bake for 20 minutes. Turn the oven off and, with the oven door ajar, let the biscotti sit another 10 minutes. Place on a rack to cool before icing.

Meanwhile, make the icing. Melt the chocolate and butter in the top of a double boiler over simmering water or in the microwave. Add the liqueur and stir.

When the biscotti are cool, drip or drizzle a scant teaspoon of chocolate icing along the cut side of each biscotti. Refrigerate to set the icing, about 2 hours.

DUTCH ALMOND COOKIES

In Dutch, these are called amandel koekjes. The word "cookie" comes from the Dutch "koekje," meaning "small cake." Almond paste is available at most supermarkets.

YIELD | 24 COOKIES

1½   cups all-purpose flour

1   teaspoon baking soda

8   tablespoons (1 cup) room-temperature unsalted butter, sliced + more for greasing

½   cup superfine sugar

½   cup packed brown sugar

2   large eggs, lightly beaten

1   cup almond paste, loosely crumbled

½   cup sliced almonds

Preheat the oven to 325°F. Butter two baking sheets.

In a small bowl, using a fork, stir together the flour and baking soda.

In a bowl large enough to hold all the ingredients, cream the 1 cup butter with an electric mixer and gradually beat in the sugars. Beat in the eggs. Mix in the flour mixture and incorporate the almond paste. Mix until smooth, then fold in the almonds. Using about 2 teaspoonfuls for each cookie, drop the batter 2 inches apart on the prepared baking sheets.

Bake until lightly browned, about 15 minutes. Transfer to a cake rack and let cool completely. Store in an airtight container for up to 1 week.

PIES AND CAKES

BUNDT CAKES AND POUND CAKES, sheet cakes, shortcakes, and roulades are all "a piece of cake" to make, and they travel well. Sweet loaves can be sliced and carried on a tray tightly covered with plastic wrap. For layer cakes, layers can be made in advance, frozen (up to 2 months), and filled, frosted, and decorated when you want. You can also carry frosting in a disposable container to decorate at your destination. Pie shells made from gingersnaps, graham crackers, or chocolate wafers can be filled with a variety of sweets at home or just before eating.

I have always preferred making fruit tarts to pies because, though they look fancier, they're easier to make. When I was in Seattle and cherries were in season, I knew it was time to learn to make a real pie in a double crust. I now substitute pitted cherries for strawberries in rhubarb recipes. That said, any fruit in season, cut and roasted till the natural sugars caramelize, or raw and lightly macerated to enhance the flavors, makes a great base for desserts.

Use fruit in season, or freeze your own in the easiest way possible. Berries, dusted with sugar and placed in a freezer bag in a thin layer, can be frozen for months. Please don't use "artificial" anything. Use pure vanilla extract or vanilla beans. The same is true for almond extract and maple syrup. The supplies you need for baking are basic. Two 9-inch round cake pans, two 9-inch pie pans, one 13-by-9-inch sheet cake pan, one 17-by-12-inch jelly-roll pan, 10-inch pie pan, and 9-inch and 12-inch tart pans with removable bottoms will get you through most recipes. If you think you'll be making angel food cake more than once, consider purchasing a 10-inch springform pan, a 9-inch tube pan, and an angel food cake pan with legs.

Any of these cakes and pies can be served on your own serving dish or your host's. Some people I know enjoy finding single plates and platters at flea markets and yard sales that they can pass along to their hosts.

A IS FOR APPLE PIE

YIELD | 10 SERVINGS

1	unbaked double 10-inch piecrust (page 223)	¼	cup brown sugar
8	medium–large crisp, slightly tart assorted apples, such as Macoun, McIntosh, and Granny Smith	1½	teaspoons ground cinnamon
1–2	tablespoons fresh lemon juice	¾	cup + 2 tablespoons granulated sugar, or to taste
4	tablespoons unsalted butter	3	tablespoons instant flour
		2	tablespoons heavy cream

Preheat the oven to 425°F. Place a baking sheet or foil-topped baking stone in the oven. (This catches drips and also gives the pie a hot surface on which to bake, preventing a soggy bottom crust.) Place the bottom half of the piecrust in a 10-inch pie pan.

Wash and dry the apples, then core and peel them. Cut into ½-inch-thick slices. You don't want them to be too thin.

In a large bowl, mix the apples with the lemon juice. Heat the butter in a large heavy skillet over medium heat and sauté the apple slices until golden at the edges, about 5 minutes. Remove from the heat.

Stir the brown sugar, cinnamon, and the ¾ cup granulated sugar into the hot apples, sprinkle with the flour, and stir. Let cool to room temperature.

Transfer the apple mixture to the piecrust and carefully place the rolled-out top crust on top. Pinch the edges together, making a thick, fluted edge.

With a single-sided safety razor blade, slit several vents in the top crust. Brush with the cream and sprinkle with the remaining 2 tablespoons granulated sugar. Wrap the edge of the crust in foil to cover the seam. Bake for 10 minutes, then reduce the heat to 375°F and bake until the crust is golden brown and the juice is bubbling at the vents, about 40 minutes. Remove the foil during the last 15 minutes of baking. If you think your oven heat is very uneven, turn the pie from front to back halfway through the baking time.

Remove the pie to a cake rack and cool at least 1½ hours before serving. Serve warm or at room temperature, with extra-sharp cheddar cheese or vanilla or cinnamon ice cream.

LEMON MERINGUE PIE

Meyer lemons, slightly sweeter than regular lemons and with a hint of mandarin orange, give this classic a "new" taste.

YIELD | 10 SERVINGS

Pie

1	extra-large egg
4	extra-large egg yolks
1	cup granulated sugar if using Meyer lemons, or 1¼ cups for regular lemons
	Juice of 3 Meyer or regular lemons

3	tablespoons unsalted butter, sliced, at room temperature
1	tablespoon lemon zest (see page 262)
1	baked and cooled double 10-inch piecrust (see page 223)*

*Remaining pie dough can be used for tartlets.

Meringue

4	extra-large egg whites, at room temperature
¼	teaspoon + ⅛ teaspoon cream of tartar

½	cup superfine sugar

Preheat the oven to 375°F, or simply leave the oven on if you have just baked the piecrust.

To make the pie: In a heavy saucepan, beat together the egg, egg yolks, and granulated sugar. Place over low heat and stir in the lemon juice. Stir in the butter and gradually increase the heat to medium. Stir constantly until the mixture thickens. If it coats the back of a wooden spoon and leaves a clear line when you draw your finger through it, it is thick enough.

Remove from the heat, stir in the lemon zest, and let rest for 5 minutes, stirring once or twice. With a rubber spatula, spread the filling from edge to edge in the piecrust.

Bake until the filling is set, 15 minutes. Remove the pie from the oven. Increase the oven temperature to 425°F.

(continued)

To make the meringue: In a large clean bowl, beat the egg whites with an electric mixer until foamy. Gradually add the cream of tartar and superfine sugar and beat until stiff, shiny peaks form.

To assemble and bake the pie: With the aid of a rubber spatula, mound meringue over the pie and, leaving the highest portion in the middle, gently spread it from edge to edge, covering all of the filling. Bake until lightly browned, 4 to 6 minutes. Do not overbake, or the meringue will shrink and toughen.

Let cool completely, at least 2 to 3 hours. This pie is best not refrigerated, as the texture of the meringue will change. However, most people are used to these pies being chilled, so do so if it is more convenient.

SWEET AND TART CHERRY PIE

This recipe really is easy as pie. If you want to make it a little more aromatic, you might add a splash of orange flower water or culinary rose water.

YIELD | ONE 10-INCH PIE

1	unbaked double 10-inch piecrust (page 223)
3	cups (about 1½ pints) sweet cherries, pitted
3	cups (about 1½ pints) tart cherries, pitted
1	cup sugar, or to taste
¾	teaspoon ground cinnamon
½	teaspoon ground nutmeg
1	teaspoon pure almond or vanilla extract
5	tablespoons instant tapioca
2	tablespoons unsalted butter

Preheat the oven to 375°F. Place the bottom half of the piecrust in a 10-inch pie pan.

Pick over the cherries to see if there are any pits or chips still attached.

In a large bowl, mix the cherries and sugar. Let stand for 15 minutes. Stir in the cinnamon, nutmeg, and almond or vanilla extract, then the tapioca. Pour into the piecrust and dot with the butter. Cover loosely with the top crust and crimp the edges to seal by pinching with your fingers. With a single-edged safety razor, cut a few decorative slits to allow steam to escape.

Bake for 45 minutes. Some juices will bubble through. If it looks like the rim is getting too brown, cover the edge with a ring of folded foil. Let cool completely before serving.

PUMPKIN PIE

"Hurrah for the fun! Is the pudding done? Hurrah for the pumpkin pie!" (from "Over the River")

YIELD | 10 SERVINGS

4	cups fresh pumpkin puree from two 8- to 10-inch pie pumpkins or canned pumpkin	1	teaspoon ground cinnamon	
1	cup (1½ cups, if using canned pumpkin) heavy cream	½	teaspoon ground ginger	
		½	teaspoon ground nutmeg	
3	egg yolks, lightly beaten	¼	teaspoon ground cloves	
¾	cup brown sugar	¼	teaspoon freshly ground pepper	
3	tablespoons unsalted butter, melted	1	unbaked 9-inch deep-dish piecrust (page 223)*	
1	teaspoon pure vanilla extract			

Remaining pie dough can be used for tartlets

Preheat the oven to 350°F.

If using fresh pumpkins, scrub them with water only, no soap. Halve them and remove the seeds and stringy insides. Bake for 1½ hours, until more than fork-tender. Alternatively, peel, cube, and boil on the stove top until fork-tender, about 20 minutes. Puree the cooked pumpkin with an immersion blender or food processor. Blend in the cream.

In a large bowl, whisk the egg yolks with the sugar and butter. Whisk in the vanilla and spices, then fold in the pumpkin-cream blend. Pour into the piecrust and spread from edge to edge with a rubber spatula.

Bake until the edges of the filling start to brown, about 1 hour 10 minutes. If the rim of the piecrust looks like it is getting too brown after 30 minutes, cover with foil.

Remove from the oven and let cool. The filling will set more as the pie cools.

BANANA RUM TART

YIELD | ONE 12-INCH TART (10 TO 12 SERVINGS)

Pastry Cream

2	cups whole milk	6	egg yolks
⅓	cup instant flour	½	teaspoon vanilla
6	tablespoons superfine sugar	2	tablespoons unsalted butter

Tart

1	prebaked 12-inch tart shell (see page 221)	6	firm, ripe bananas, sliced thin
5	tablespoons unsalted butter	⅓	cup dark rum
⅓	cup sugar	1¼	cups apple or guava jelly
3	tablespoons fresh lime juice	2	tablespoons kirsch, or any clear liqueur

To make the pastry cream: In a saucepan over medium heat, bring the milk to just below boiling. Remove from the heat. In another saucepan, mix the flour, sugar, and egg yolks together. Slowly whisk the hot milk into the flour mixture over medium-low heat. Whisk continuously until the cream is smooth and thick, about 5 minutes. Remove from the heat. With a rubber spatula, stir in the vanilla and butter until creamy. Cool. The pastry cream may be covered and refrigerated for 24 hours.

To make the tart: Spoon the cooled pastry cream into the tart shell and gently smooth with a rubber spatula.

Heat 3 tablespoons of the butter in a heavy skillet over medium-low heat. Stir in the sugar and lime juice, and cook until golden brown, about 4 minutes. Stir the bananas into the butter mixture for 2 minutes to coat evenly. Remove from the heat and stir in the rum. With the aid of a spoon and a rubber spatula, spread the bananas over the pastry cream. Let cool.

For the glaze, melt the jelly and remaining 2 tablespoons of the butter in a small heavy pan, stirring constantly. Add the kirsch. Drizzle the glaze over the tart.

PECAN TART

Over the years, more people have asked me for this recipe than for any other. Okay, folks, here it is. The secret is out: NO corn syrup. This tart develops a unique custardy texture all its own that contrasts with the crisp crust and pecans. No substitutions. I can't tell you why, but pecans are the nuts of choice for this one.

YIELD | 9-INCH TART, 6 TO 8 SERVINGS; 12-INCH TART, 10 TO 12 SERVINGS

9-inch tart

1	partially baked 9-inch tart shell (recipe follows)	⅓	cup water
		2	tablespoons unsalted butter
1	large egg	1	teaspoon pure vanilla extract
1	large egg yolk	2	cups pecan halves
1½	cups light brown sugar		

12-inch tart

1	partially baked 12-inch tart shell	1	cup water
2	large eggs	4	tablespoons unsalted butter
3	large egg yolks	1½	teaspoons pure vanilla extract
3	cups light brown sugar	3	cups pecan halves

Preheat the oven to 350°F. Place a foil-lined baking sheet on the lowest shelf of the oven in case the filling bubbles over. Set a rack in the middle of the oven for baking the pecan tart. Set out the partially baked tart shell.

In a large bowl, whisk the egg(s) and egg yolks together.

In a heavy saucepan over medium-high heat, combine the brown sugar and water. Heat until the sugar dissolves, stirring constantly. Lower the heat to medium and bring to a slow boil. Maintain for 2 to 3 minutes, then stir in the butter and vanilla. In a slow stream, pour the syrup into the eggs, whisking constantly. Add the pecans and mix until fully coated. Carefully pour into the tart shell to within ¼ inch of the top.

Bake for 35 minutes, or until a cake tester comes out clean. Remove to a cake rack and let cool completely before removing the tart pan ring. It may be sticky, so have patience. You may need to use a narrow paring knife if sugar has gotten between the shell and pan.

RELIABLE TART SHELLS

A tart is basically a shallow open-faced pie. It's made in a tart pan, which has straight (not sloped) fluted sides. Metal tart pans have removable bottoms. This recipe can be doubled to make two 9-inch tart shells or one 12-inch tart shell.

YIELD | ONE 9-INCH TART SHELL

1 cup all-purpose flour + more for dusting

6 tablespoons unsalted butter, diced and frozen + more for greasing

2 tablespoons sugar

1 egg yolk

1–2 tablespoons ice water

Pinch of salt

Preheat the oven to 375°F. Lightly butter a 9-inch tart pan with a removable bottom and dust with flour.

Place the 1 cup flour and the 6 tablespoons butter in a food processor fitted with a metal blade and pulse for 4 seconds. Add the sugar and egg yolk and pulse for 5 seconds. Add 1 tablespoon of the ice water and the salt and pulse until the dough forms a solid ball. If a ball doesn't start forming after a few pulses, add the second tablespoon of water.

Remove the dough from the processor, flatten slightly, cover with plastic wrap, and let rest for 30 minutes before proceeding.

Using a rolling pin, shape the dough into a thick circle, transfer it to the prepared tart pan, and press it out with your fingers, pushing the dough into the side of the pan. Smooth the dough evenly and prick in several places with a sharp-tined fork.

Line the shell with parchment paper and fill with pie weights or beans. Bake for 15 minutes. Remove from the oven to a level cooling rack. Remove the weights and parchment paper and proceed with a recipe that calls for a partially baked shell.

If you are using a filling that will not be baked, return the tart to the oven until golden brown, an additional 10 minutes. Let cool completely on the rack and add the prepared cold filling. This shell will be completely baked.

The shells can be cooled, left on the removable metal bottom of the tart pan, covered well with plastic wrap, and refrigerated for 2 days or frozen for up to 1 month.

PIECRUSTS

Single 9-Inch Crust

1⅓   cups all-purpose flour + more for
      dusting

½   teaspoon salt

2   tablespoons Crisco Stick

2   tablespoons sweet unsalted butter

3   tablespoons ice water

In a bowl large enough to hold all the ingredients, mix the 1⅓ cups flour and salt with a fork.

Using a pastry blender or two knives, cut in the Crisco and butter until the mixture is the texture of coarse meal. Sprinkle with the water, 1 tablespoon at a time. Toss lightly with a fork until the dough will form a ball. Press into a 5-inch disk and flour lightly.

For a single crust, roll the dough between sheets of waxed paper (or a designated silicone surface) 1½ inches larger than an inverted 9-inch pie plate. Using a flour shaker, dust the dough as you roll it out. Peel off the top sheet and gently fold in half, then in quarters. Open onto a pie plate. Peel off the other sheet and press dough gently with your fingertips to fit. Fold the edge under. Pinch a fluted edge with your fingertips.

To make a recipe calling for a single unbaked crust: Follow as directed in the recipe you are making.

To make a recipe calling for a prebaked piecrust: Heat the oven to 425°F. Thoroughly prick the bottom and sides of the crust with a fork (being careful not to tear the dough) at least 25 times to prevent shrinking.

Line the pastry with parchment paper or aluminum foil and lay some pastry weights over all. Bake for 10 minutes. Remove the pastry from the oven, but do not turn off the oven. Remove the weights and liner and return to the oven until golden brown, 3 to 5 minutes. Follow the pie recipe you are making for further baking.

Double 9-Inch Crust, Double 9-Inch Deep Dish Crust, or Double 10-Inch Crust

Double 9-inch crust

2	cups all-purpose flour	5	tablespoons sweet unsalted butter
1	teaspoon salt	5	tablespoons ice water
5	tablespoons Crisco Stick		

Double 9-inch deep dish or Double 10-inch crust

2⅔	cups all-purpose flour	8	tablespoons sweet unsalted butter
1	teaspoon salt	7–8	tablespoons ice water
8	tablespoons Crisco Stick		

In a bowl large enough to hold all the ingredients, mix the flour and salt with a fork.

Using a pastry blender or two knives, cut in the Crisco and butter until the mixture is the texture of coarse meal. Sprinkle with the water, 1 tablespoon at a time. Toss lightly with a fork until the dough forms a ball. Divide in half, press into two 5- to 6-inch disks, and flour lightly.

Roll each disk between sheets of waxed paper (or a designated silicone surface) 1½ inches larger than inverted pie plate. For a 9-inch deep-dish pie, roll dough 2½ inches larger than pan. Using a flour shaker, dust the dough as you roll it out.

Peel off the top sheet of waxed paper from one of the discs and gently fold the dough in half, then quarters. Open onto a pie plate. Peel off the other sheet and press the dough gently with your fingertips to fit.

Add the desired filling to the unbaked piecrust.

Remove the top sheet of waxed paper from the top crust. Lift the crust loosely onto the filled pie, then remove the other sheet of paper. Trim to ½ inch beyond the edge of the pie plate. Fold the top edge under the bottom crust. Pinch a fluted edge together with your fingertips, a pie crimper, or the tines of a fork. Cut slits in the top crust to allow steam to escape.

Bake according to recipe instructions.

SUMMER STRAWBERRY SHORTCAKE

This classic summer crowd-pleaser is also very tasty with Rhubarb-Cherry Topping (page 226).

YIELD | 12 SERVINGS

Cake

2	cups self-rising flour	⅔	cup whole milk
⅔	cup granulated sugar	1	teaspoon pure vanilla extract
⅔	cup unsalted butter, sliced + more for greasing	1	jumbo egg, lightly beaten

Topping

4	cups (about 2 pints) strawberries	1	teaspoon pure vanilla extract
½	cup granulated sugar	1	tablespoon superfine sugar
½	pint (1 cup) heavy cream		Mint leaves, for garnish

Preheat the oven to 375°F. Butter only the bottom of a 13-by-9½-by-1-inch sheet pan.

To make the cake: In a large bowl, mix the flour and sugar. Cut in the ⅔ cup butter with a pastry blender or two butter knives until the mixture resembles coarse flakes. Mix in the milk, vanilla, and egg just until the batter is evenly moistened. Don't over-mix. Spread in the prepared pan. Bake until the top is golden brown and a cake tester comes out clean, 20 to 25 minutes.

To make the topping: Rinse the strawberries in cold water and dry on paper towels. Hull and quarter into a bowl. Sprinkle with the granulated sugar, stir, and let macerate. Cover and refrigerate until ready to use.

In a cold medium bowl, using a balloon or electric mixer on medium-high speed, whip the cream with the vanilla and superfine sugar until quite thick. Cover and refrigerate until ready to use.

To assemble and serve the shortcake: Cut the cake into 12 squares. Top with strawberries, a dollop of the whipped cream, and mint leaves. These can be placed on a large platter or individual dessert plates.

(continued)

RHUBARB–CHERRY TOPPING

This also makes a great topping for sorbet or vanilla ice cream.

¾ cup water

1¼ cups sugar, or to taste

2 pounds rhubarb, leaves removed but not the strings, sliced into 1½-inch pieces

2 cups (about ¾ pounds, or 1 pint) cherries, pitted

3–4 tablespoons instant tapioca

In a medium-heavy saucepan combine the water, sugar, and rhubarb. Bring to the boiling point over medium heat, reduce the heat, and simmer for 10 minutes. Add the cherries, stir, and simmer for another 5 minutes. Sprinkle in the tapioca and stir until dissolved.

Remove from the heat and let cool. Place in a covered refrigerator dish until ready to serve, up to 3 days.

VANILLA-POPPY SEED POUND CAKE

YIELD | 20 SERVINGS

Cake

2	cups cake flour		¼	cup light brown sugar
1	teaspoon baking powder		1	tablespoon pure vanilla extract
½	teaspoon salt		4	large eggs, lightly beaten
1	cup (8 ounces) unsalted butter + more for greasing		3	tablespoons poppy seeds
1	cup granulated sugar			

Glaze

½	cup granulated sugar		1	teaspoon pure vanilla extract
⅓	cup water		1	tablespoon poppy seeds (optional)

Preheat the oven to 350°F. Lightly butter the bottom and sides of a 10-inch tube pan, preferably springform.

To make the cake: In a medium bowl, stir together the flour, baking powder, and salt.

In a large bowl, using an electric mixer, cream the 1 cup butter, then add the sugars and vanilla. Alternate beating in the eggs and the flour mixture. Stir in the poppy seeds, if using, in a stream. Pour the batter into the prepared pan and smooth lightly with a rubber spatula.

Bake in the bottom third of the oven for 1 hour 10 minutes, or until the top is lightly browned and a cake tester comes out clean. Let cool in the pan for 15 minutes, then turn the cake out on a cake rack over waxed paper. With a cake tester or toothpick, pierce the cake on the top and sides.

To make the glaze: In a small saucepan, heat the sugar and water over medium-low heat just to the boiling point, stirring, until the sugar is dissolved. Remove from the heat and stir in the vanilla and poppy seeds, if using.

To assemble the cake: Drip the glaze over the top and sides of the cake, spreading with a brush as you do. Gently tilt the cake as you cover the sides. Let the cake cool completely before serving.

PEANUT BUTTER LAYER CAKE

I know people who don't like to use the freezer. I was one of them. However, in a busy life, if you enjoy baking from scratch, the freezer is a terrific time-saving tool. This cake can be made from start to finish and served the same day or the next—or the layers can be baked, cooled thoroughly, wrapped in plastic wrap, and frozen for several weeks before thawing and assembling.

YIELD | ONE 9-INCH CAKE (12 SLICES)

Cake Layers

2½	cups all-purpose flour + more for dusting		1	cup peanut butter, at room temperature
1	tablespoon baking powder		6	eggs
½	teaspoon sea salt		2	teaspoons pure vanilla extract
8	tablespoons (½ cup) unsalted butter, sliced, at room temperature + more for greasing		1	cup sour cream
			1	cup hot water
2½	cups light brown sugar			

Frosting

3	egg whites		6	ounces milk chocolate, melted
¾	cup superfine sugar		1½	cups roasted peanuts, coarsely chopped
1	cup (8 ounces) unsalted butter, sliced, at room temperature			

To make the cake: Preheat the oven to 350°F. Lightly butter and dust with flour two 9-inch cake pans, preferably 2 inches deep.

In a small bowl, using a fork, stir together the 2½ cups flour, baking powder, and salt.

In a stand mixer with a paddle attachment or a large bowl and electric mixer, on medium to medium-high speed, cream together the ½ cup butter, brown sugar, and peanut butter. Add the eggs and vanilla and keep beating until well mixed. Incorporate the flour mixture, beat in the sour cream and water. Divide the batter among the prepared pans and bake until a cake tester comes out clean, about 35 minutes. Cool the cake in the pans on a cake rack for 10 minutes. Remove the cake from the pans and continue cooling. If the layers are domed, trim them horizontally so they're level for stacking.

To make the frosting: Simmer 2 inches of water in the bottom of a double boiler.

In a mixing bowl or the top of double boiler, whisk the egg whites and sugar until blended. Place over simmering water and whisk until the mixture is hot and the sugar dissolved. Turn off the heat and remove the mixing bowl from the pan of water.

Using an electric mixer, beat the mixture on high speed until thick and cool, about 5 minutes. Gradually beat in the butter and chocolate at medium speed until well incorporated.

To assemble the cake: Spread the frosting over each cake layer, stack them, then coat the top and sides generously. Sprinkle the peanuts over all. Refrigerate for at least 1 hour to set the buttercream. Serve at room temperature.

MEXICAN CHOCOLATE CAKE

The 15th of September is Mexico's true Independence Day and celebrates its separation from Spain in 1810. On May 5, 1862, the region of Puebla in Mexico won a huge victory against the French. Traditionally a local holiday, it has grown into an annual celebration of Mexican popular culture, with food and drink and music. Cinco de Mayo has become an American tradition celebrated more north of the Mexican border than south.

YIELD | 12 SERVINGS

Cake

1½	cups cake flour
1¼	cups sugar
⅔	cup cocoa or dark chocolate powder
1	teaspoon baking powder
1	teaspoon baking soda
2	teaspoons ground cinnamon
½	teaspoon cayenne pepper
1	teaspoon ancho chili powder
3	large eggs, lightly beaten

2	teaspoons pure vanilla extract
5	tablespoons corn, canola, or safflower oil
½	cup milk
1	tablespoon white vinegar
½	cup red jalapeño pepper jelly, such as Goya
2	tablespoons unsalted butter + more for greasing

Frosting

4	ounces dark chocolate, chopped
1	teaspoon ground cinnamon
3	tablespoons heavy cream
2	tablespoons unsalted butter

½	teaspoon pure vanilla extract
12	beautiful whole small, long red and green chili peppers, such as Fresno, Colorado, or Anaheim, for decoration

Cinnamon Whipped Cream

1	cup (½ pint) heavy whipping cream
1	tablespoon superfine sugar

¼	teaspoon pure vanilla extract
½	teaspoon cinnamon

(continued)

Preheat the oven to 350°F. Butter the bottom and sides of a 9-inch cake pan. Line the bottom with buttered parchment paper.

To make the cake: In a medium bowl, lightly stir the flour, sugar, cocoa or chocolate powder, baking powder, baking soda, cinnamon, cayenne, and chili powder with a fork.

In a large bowl, beat the eggs with an electric mixer until light and creamy. Beat in the vanilla and oil then mix in the flour-cocoa mixture, milk, and vinegar.

Pour into the prepared pan and bake for 30 minutes. Lower the oven temperature to 300° and bake until a cake tester comes out clean, about 25 minutes more.

Cool in the pan on a cake rack for 15 to 20 minutes. The cake will still be warm. Remove from the pan, turn upside down on a wire rack, and remove the parchment paper. Leave flat side up on the wire rack.

In a small saucepan, melt the jelly and 2 tablespoons butter. Spread on the top and sides of the cake while warm. Let cool completely, then cover the cake with the chocolate frosting.

To make the frosting: Place the chocolate, cinnamon, cream, and butter in the top of a double boiler. Set over simmering water until melted. Whisk until well blended and shiny. Remove from the heat and stir in the vanilla. When room temperature, frost the cake. Refrigerate.

To make the cinnamon whipped cream: Whip the cream in a medium-large bowl with an electric mixer on medium-high or with a balloon whisk. As it thickens, add the sugar, vanilla, and cinnamon. When stiff peaks form, cover the bowl with plastic wrap and refrigerate. Transfer to a serving bowl when ready to serve.

To serve the dish: Serve at room temperature with the cinnamon whipped cream in a serving bowl alongside. Garnish with the brightly colored peppers. Make sure to tell people that they are not marzipan. Or, if you are especially ambitious, make them from marzipan.

POTLUCK NOTE | *This cake can be made and kept in the refrigerator for several days before serving. When it is fully iced, the icing seals it and it will stay moist.*

BLUEBERRY CAKE

1	cup sugar	2	teaspoons baking powder
¼	cup water	½	teaspoon salt
1	tablespoon fresh lemon juice	½	teaspoon ground cinnamon
1	teaspoon instant tapioca or cornstarch	1	egg
		½	cup milk
2½	cups (about 1½ pints) blueberries, rinsed and dried	6	tablespoons unsalted butter, sliced, at room temperature + more for greasing
	Grated zest of ½ lemon (see page 262)	1	teaspoon pure vanilla extract
1¼	cups all-purpose flour		

Preheat the oven to 375°F. Lightly butter a 9-inch baking pan.

In a medium saucepan over medium-low heat, stir together ½ cup of the sugar, water, lemon juice, and tapioca. Bring to a low boil and stir in the blueberries. Bring to a low boil again, stir, remove from the heat, and stir in the lemon zest.

In a small bowl, mix together the flour, baking powder, salt, and cinnamon.

In a mixing bowl, using an electric mixer at medium speed, beat the egg, milk, 6 table-spoons butter, vanilla, and the remaining ½ cup sugar. Gradually mix in the flour mixture.

Pour the batter into the prepared baking pan and lightly spread from edge to edge with a rubber spatula. Pour the blueberry mixture in an even layer over the batter.

Bake until a cake tester comes out clean, about 30 minutes.

Let cool for 1 hour before serving, or cool completely, cover with plastic wrap, and refrigerate for up to 24 hours. Bring to room temperature before serving.

CHOCOLATE–BUTTERMILK AMERICAN FLAG CAKE

Every summer, versions of this cake are presented at Fourth of July celebrations. This one uses a cake recipe that is tasty with any topping. Clearly, the white frosting can be a blank canvas for your imagination. Toasted coconut mixed with chopped toasted walnuts makes a delicious replacement for the berries when they are out of season.

YIELD | 12 TO 16 SERVINGS

Cake

½	cup buttermilk
1	teaspoon baking soda
¼	cup unsweetened cocoa powder
1	teaspoon ground cinnamon
1	cup water
8	tablespoons (½ cup) unsalted butter, sliced and softened + more for greasing
½	cup canola or safflower oil
1	teaspoon pure vanilla extract
2	large eggs
2	cups all-purpose flour + more for dusting
2	cups granulated sugar

Frosting

2	packages (8 ounces each) cream cheese, softened
3	tablespoons heavy cream
2	tablespoons superfine sugar
8	ounces marshmallow cream
1	cup (about ½ pint) blueberries, rinsed and dried
3	cups (about 1½ pints) raspberries or strawberry halves, rinsed and dried

To make the cake: Preheat the oven to 350°F. Lightly butter and flour a 13-by-9-inch oven-to-table baking pan.

In a small bowl, mix together the buttermilk and baking soda.

In a medium saucepan over medium heat, stir together the cocoa, cinnamon, water, the 8 tablespoons butter, and oil. Bring to the boiling point, stirring constantly. Remove from the heat and stir in the vanilla and the buttermilk mixture. Beat in the eggs, then beat in the 2 cups flour and sugar until smooth. Pour into the prepared pan.

Bake until a cake tester comes out clean, 15 to 20 minutes. Let cool in the pan.

When the cake is completely cool, it can be covered and refrigerated for up to 2 days before frosting and decorating.

To make the frosting: In a medium bowl, combine the cream cheese, heavy cream, and sugar, then mix in the marshmallow cream by hand or with an electric mixer, beating until smooth and fluffy. Spread over the cooled cake. Refrigerate for 1½ hours before decorating.

To decorate the cake: Arrange the blueberries in a 5-inch square in the upper left corner of the cake to make the blue field of the flag. Starting and ending at the edges of the cake, arrange seven horizontal rows of raspberries, leaving white stripes in between.

CAROL'S OLD-FASHIONED GINGERBREAD

Carol is one of the best bakers I know. The first time I tasted this cake, she had carried all the ingredients in plastic storage bags in a canvas tote bag. The flour was in one plastic bag; the baking soda, spices, and salt in another; and the sugar in a third. She transported the butter and cream in a thermal container and also brought along her own 8-by-8-inch baking dish and a bowl. The results were perfect.

YIELD | 16 TWO-INCH SQUARES

2	cups all-purpose flour	⅓	cup sugar
2	teaspoons baking soda	1	large egg
2¼	teaspoons ground ginger	¾	cup molasses
½	teaspoon ground cinnamon	¾	cup cold water
¼	teaspoon ground cloves	¼	cup pure maple syrup
	Pinch of salt	½	pint (1 cup) heavy cream, whipped
5	tablespoons unsalted butter, sliced, at room temperature + more for greasing		

Preheat the oven to 350°F. Lightly butter an 8-by-8-inch cake pan.

In a small bowl, using a fork, blend the flour, baking soda, spices, and salt.

In a large mixing bowl, using an electric mixer, cream the 5 tablespoons butter and sugar until light and fluffy. Add the egg and beat until well incorporated. Scrape down the sides of the bowl and drizzle in the molasses, beating constantly. Add half of the flour mixture and mix until combined, then mix in the rest. Slowly pour in the cold water and stir until well incorporated. Pour the batter into the prepared cake pan.

Bake until a cake tester comes out clean, about 35 minutes. Place the pan on a cooling rack for at least 1 hour.

Mix the maple syrup into the whipped cream and serve with cake squares.

POTLUCK NOTE | *In the fall, stewed apples and pears are a welcome accompaniment to squares of gingerbread and maple cream.*

PUMPKIN CHEESECAKE
WITH GINGER–PECAN CRUST

This variation on a traditional pumpkin pie is a welcome treat.

YIELD | 12 SERVINGS

Crust

1½	cups crumbled gingersnaps (about 30 cookies)	7	tablespoons unsalted butter, melted + more for greasing
½	cup finely chopped pecans	¼	cup superfine sugar

Filling

3	packages (8 ounces each) cream cheese, at room temperature	½	teaspoon ground nutmeg
1	can (15 ounces) pumpkin puree	3	tablespoons crystallized ginger, minced
4	large egg yolks, lightly beaten	⅓	cup heavy cream
1½	cups superfine sugar	2	tablespoons cornstarch
1	teaspoon ground cinnamon	2	teaspoons pure vanilla extract

Preheat the oven to 400°F. Generously butter a 10-inch springform pan. Wrap foil around the outside bottom of the pan and up the sides a bit to cover and waterproof the seams. Simmer 6 cups of water in a kettle over medium heat.

To make the crust: In a medium bowl, mix the gingersnaps, pecans, the 7 tablespoons butter, and sugar. Press on the bottom and 1½ inches up the inside of the prepared pan. Chill in the refrigerator for 30 minutes, then bake for 10 minutes. Remove to a cake rack to cool. Maintain the oven heat.

To make the filling: In a large bowl or the bowl of a stand mixer, beat the cream cheese, pumpkin, egg yolks, and sugar at medium speed. When smooth and creamy, add the cinnamon, nutmeg, and ginger. Beat in the cream and cornstarch and add the vanilla.

(continued)

Pour the cheesecake mixture into the crust and place in a roasting pan. Carefully pour the hot water into the roasting pan so that it reaches no more than halfway up the sides of the springform pan.

Place the roasting pan on the center shelf of the oven. Reduce the heat to 350°F and bake for 1 hour 10 minutes. The center of the cheesecake should still look a bit custard-like.

Remove the cheesecake from the roasting pan, remove the foil, and place on a cake rack to cool for 2 hours. Chill in the refrigerator for at least 4 hours. If the cake is not being served immediately, cover the top of the springform pan with plastic wrap, being sure to keep the plastic from touching the top of the cake.

BREADS, ROLLS, AND MUFFINS

MEALS FOR WHICH different people make different courses are the ideal occasions to try baking bread. Baking is such a luxury in a busy life that attention should be paid to the quality of the ingredients. The first time may be the hardest but it also might be the most fun.

As far as equipment goes, "less is more" and "know thyself" are both good axioms. If you are going to be baking for a crowd, two of everything, including measuring spoons and measuring cup sets, is a good idea. Stock your kitchen with two 9-by-5-inch loaf pans; two baking sheets; two cake racks; one muffin tin for 12 regular-size muffins and one for mini-size muffins. Various bowls for mixing, proofing, and rising are handy. Pyrex or other transparent heatproof measuring pitchers are very useful in small, medium, and large sizes. Two wooden spoons, balloon whisks, rubber spatulas, a pastry blender and a package of one-side "safety" razor blades or a lame for slashing the crust of some yeast breads are practical. Thin wooden skewers to use as cake testers, a small spray bottle to moisten loaves and a good-sized trivet are helpful.

I recommend oven mitts that go halfway up your arm. More burns are caused by contact with the oven than with a pan.

If I had to recommend one luxury, it would be a stand mixer with a paddle and dough hook attachment. I know many people who bake a lot without one, using only a sturdy electric handheld mixer.

When you have seen as many professional kitchens as I have, you realize that terrific food is being made under the most diverse conditions all over the world.

Poppy Seed Rolls (opposite)
Parker House Rolls (page 242)

POPPY SEED ROLLS

These buns are quite good, they're easy to make, and they freeze well, so you can have them whenever you're in the mood.

YIELD | 16 ROLLS

2	packages active dry yeast (½ ounce)	1½	teaspoons sea salt
1	teaspoon sugar	5	cups bread flour
½	cup warm water	1	egg white, beaten
2	cups low-fat milk	2	tablespoons poppy seeds
2	tablespoons unsalted butter + more for greasing		

Butter a large mixing bowl and lightly butter a baking sheet.

In a large bowl, dissolve the yeast and sugar in the warm water and let stand for 5 minutes, or until it foams.

In a small saucepan over medium heat, scald the milk and remove from the heat. Add the 2 tablespoons butter and bring to room temperature. Stir the milk mixture and salt into the yeast mixture. Beat in 2 cups of the flour, then gradually add the remaining 3 cups.

Turn out the dough onto a lightly floured work surface and knead until smooth and elastic, about 10 minutes. Place the dough in the prepared mixing bowl and turn it to coat with a film of butter. Cover with a damp tea towel and let rise for 2 hours. Push the dough down and turn out onto a lightly buttered surface. Divide into four parts, then into four again. Roll each section into a round ball with a flat bottom. Place on the prepared baking sheet, cover, and let rise for 1 hour.

Preheat the oven to 375°F. Brush the tops of the rolls with the egg white and sprinkle with the poppy seeds. Bake until golden brown, about 15 minutes. Remove the rolls to cake racks and let cool.

These can be served immediately or frozen for later use. Let them cool completely and seal in plastic wrap in a single layer, then place in the freezer. When you want to serve them, bring to room temperature and heat in a 350°F oven for 5 minutes.

PARKER HOUSE ROLLS

These puffy, pocket-like rolls originated in the 1870s at the Parker House Hotel in Boston, one of America's oldest continuously operating hotels. They were so popular that versions of the recipe started appearing in the 1880s.

YIELD | 24 ROLLS

2	packages active dry yeast (½ ounce)	8	tablespoons (½ cup) room-temperature unsalted butter, sliced + 3 tablespoons melted
⅓	cup sugar		
½	cup milk, warmed	1	cup hot water
5	cups all-purpose flour	2	eggs, lightly beaten
¼	teaspoon salt		

Lightly butter two 13-by-9-inch baking pans.

In a large mixing bowl, combine the yeast, sugar, and warm milk. Stir and let sit until bubbly. Add 2½ cups of the flour, salt, and room-temperature butter and beat with an electric mixer on low speed until incorporated. Gradually add the water, beat at medium speed, and add the eggs. Add another 1½ cups flour and beat until thick, about 5 minutes more. Scrape down the sides of the bowl with a rubber spatula and turn out the dough onto a clean, floured work surface. Knead in the remaining 1 cup flour for 5 minutes to make a soft, smooth dough.

Shape the dough into a ball and place in the prepared mixing bowl, turning the dough so that it is coated. Cover the bowl and let the dough rise in a warm (about 80°F) place until doubled in size, about 1½ hours. Your finger will leave a small dent when you press the dough. Push the dough down and roll out on a floured surface to a ½-inch thickness. Cover lightly with a towel and let rest for 15 minutes. Using a sharp, floured 3-inch biscuit cutter, cut the dough into 24 circles. Brush the rims with some of the melted butter and fold the circles almost in half so that the top of each looks like the flap of a pocket, and pinch the edges together. Place the rolls in the prepared pans so that they do not touch. Cover with towels and let the rolls rise for about 1 hour.

Preheat the oven to 375°F. Bake the rolls until golden brown, about 15 minutes. Remove immediately from the pan and glaze with melted butter.

CHEDDAR CHEESE BISCUITS

YIELD | 10 TO 12 BISCUITS

2¼	cups all-purpose flour
1	tablespoon sugar
1	tablespoon baking powder
1	teaspoon baking soda
½	teaspoon salt
½	teaspoon freshly ground pepper
6	tablespoons unsalted butter, sliced and chilled + more for greasing
1¼	cups coarsely grated extra-sharp cheddar cheese
1¼	cups buttermilk

Preheat the oven to 400°F. Lightly butter a large baking sheet.

In a large bowl, mix together the flour, sugar, baking powder, baking soda, salt, and pepper. Using a pastry blender or two butter knives, cut in the 6 tablespoons butter until the mixture resembles coarse meal. Slowly mix in the cheese so it doesn't clump too much. Add the buttermilk just until incorporated. Do not overmix.

Use about ⅓ cup batter for each biscuit and arrange on the baking sheet so that the biscuits do not touch. If the sheet is too small, use two. Bake until golden brown and firm to the touch, about 15 minutes.

These are best served fresh from the oven, but they can be cooled completely, wrapped in foil, and stored at room temperature for up to 12 hours. Reheat the biscuits, still wrapped in foil, in a 350°F oven for 4 minutes. Open the foil and leave in the oven for 1 minute more.

BLUEBERRY–CORN MUFFINS

If it seems like there are a lot of muffin recipes here, it's because I really, really dislike commercially made muffins. Depending on the fruit available, these fill the bill. This recipe makes 12 regular muffins or 36 mini muffins.

YIELD | 12 MUFFINS

1	cup all-purpose flour + more for dusting	1	extra-large egg
1	cup fine cornmeal	¾	cup milk
1	tablespoon baking powder	⅓	cup honey
1	teaspoon salt	⅓	cup sugar
8	tablespoons (½ cup) unsalted butter + more for greasing	2½	cups (about 1 pint) blueberries, rinsed and drained

Preheat the oven to 425°F for standard muffins, 375°F for mini muffins. Lightly butter and flour a standard 12-muffin pan or a 36-mini-muffin pan.

In a small bowl, using a fork, stir together the flour, cornmeal, baking powder, and salt.

In a medium bowl, cream the 8 tablespoons butter, then beat in the egg, milk, honey, and sugar by hand or with an electric mixer. Fold in the flour mixture and the blueberries. Spoon the batter into the muffin cups.

Bake until a cake tester comes out clean, 15 to 20 minutes. Let cool in the pan for 10 minutes, then remove the muffins to a cake rack.

RHUBARB–PECAN MUFFINS

These muffins are a bit tart and moist. When completely cooled, they can be individually wrapped and frozen. Thaw them before reheating.

YIELD | 12 MUFFINS

2	scant cups sliced fresh rhubarb (⅓-inch slices)
2	teaspoons finely grated lemon zest (see page 262)
3	teaspoons brown or granulated sugar
2	cups all-purpose flour
2	teaspoons baking powder
½	teaspoon baking soda
½	teaspoon sea salt
⅔	cup granulated sugar
1	large egg, lightly beaten
¼	cup canola or safflower oil
¾	cup milk
¾	cup chopped pecans

Preheat the oven to 350°F. Butter the bottom of a 12-muffin tin.

In a medium bowl, combine the rhubarb, lemon zest, and 3 teaspoons brown or granulated sugar.

In a large bowl, mix together the flour, baking powder, baking soda, salt, and ⅔ cup granulated sugar.

In a medium bowl, whisk together the egg, oil, and milk. Stir into the flour mixture, alternating with the rhubarb mixture. Fold in the pecans. Spoon the batter into the muffin cups.

Bake in the center of the oven until a cake tester comes out clean, about 25 minutes. Remove the pan from the oven and place on a cake rack to cool for 10 minutes. Remove the muffins from the pan and let them cool thoroughly on the cake rack.

MALTED MILK BALL MUFFINS

What can I say? Everyone likes these—except, of course, people who don't like chocolate.

YIELD | 12 MUFFINS

1½	cups all-purpose flour + more for dusting		1	large egg, beaten
½	cup unsweetened cocoa powder		¾	cup sour cream
½	cup + 1 tablespoon sugar		2	teaspoons pure vanilla extract
1	tablespoon baking powder		6	tablespoons unsweetened butter, melted and cooled + more for greasing
¼	teaspoon salt			
1	cup coarsely crushed malted milk balls (best available)		¼	cup milk

Preheat the oven to 375°F. Butter and lightly flour the bottom and sides of a 12-muffin pan or use paper liners.

In a large bowl, using a fork, combine the 1½ cups flour and cocoa powder. Stir in the sugar, baking powder, and salt, then add the malted milk balls.

In a small bowl, combine the egg, sour cream, vanilla, the 6 tablespoons butter, and milk. Add to the flour mixture and incorporate with a rubber spatula until just moistened. Do not overmix. Fill the prepared muffin tins two-thirds full.

Bake until a cake tester comes out clean, 16 to 18 minutes. Let cool in the pan on a wire rack for 5 minutes. Remove the muffins from the pan and let cool thoroughly on a cake rack.

FRANANA BANANA BREAD

This is one terrific banana bread. I have been making it for so long that people started calling it franana bread. The only variation I ever make is adding 1¼ cups of white chocolate chunks or chips or substituting them for the walnuts.

YIELD | 10 SERVINGS

1	cup whole wheat flour	1	cup honey
1	cup all-purpose flour + more for dusting	½	cup whole-milk plain yogurt
1	teaspoon baking soda	2	large eggs, lightly beaten
½	teaspoon sea salt	3	very ripe bananas, mashed
8	tablespoons (½ cup) unsalted butter, softened + more for greasing	⅔	cup coarsely chopped walnuts

Preheat the oven to 350°F. Lightly butter and flour a 9-by-5-inch loaf pan.

In a medium bowl, using a fork, stir together the flours, baking soda, and salt.

In a large bowl, beating by hand or using an electric mixer on medium speed, mix together the 8 tablespoons butter, honey, yogurt, and eggs until well incorporated. Mix in the bananas. Fold in the flour mixture and the walnuts.

Bake in the center of the oven until a cake tester comes out clean, about 1 hour. Let cool in the pan for 10 minutes, then on a cake rack until completely cool.

POTLUCK NOTE | *It is best to use unsalted butter in baking because you have better control of the flavor. If you use salted butter the recipes will be fine, however, and you don't really have to adjust the salt in the recipe. Please do not use margarine as a substitute because it is a mixture of solid and liquid fat and will affect the recipe.*

BOSTON BROWN BREAD

This bread is steamed on top of the stove in two 1-pound coffee cans. Why? No one seems certain, but my guess is that most home kitchens have had little use for cylindrical pudding molds and so made do with what was around the house.

YIELD | 12 SERVINGS

1	cup rye flour	2	cups buttermilk
1	cup whole wheat flour	1	cup molasses
1	cup medium cornmeal	1	cup currants or raisins
2	tablespoons baking soda	4	tablespoons unsalted butter, sliced, at room temperature
1	teaspoon salt		
¼	cup brown sugar		

Lightly grease two 1-pound coffee cans or cylindrical pudding molds. Start heating 2 to 3 quarts of water in a teakettle or pot.

In a medium bowl, using a fork, combine the flours, cornmeal, baking soda, salt, and sugar.

In a large bowl, beat together the buttermilk and molasses using a hand mixer or an electric mixer at medium speed. Mix in the currants or raisins, then beat in the flour mixture, followed by the butter. Pour the batter into the prepared cans, each no more than about two-thirds full. Cover each can loosely with a piece of buttered parchment or waxed paper, then top with a double fold of heavy-duty foil. Tie tightly with kitchen string or a rubber band. Trim the foil to 1½ inches from the top of each can so that the water doesn't seep underneath.

Place the cans side by side (without touching) on a rack in a Dutch oven or other heavy pan on the stove top. Pour hot water into the Dutch oven halfway up the sides of the cans. Steam over medium to medium-low heat, adding more hot water to maintain the water level, until a cake tester comes out clean, about 2 hours. Remove the cans from the water and let cool for 15 minutes before sliding the breads out of the cans.

The breads can be cooled completely, wrapped in foil, and refrigerated until needed. Heat, still wrapped in foil, in a 300°F oven, or in a colander over simmering water.

OATMEAL BREAD

This is a tasty, not overly sweet loaf. The cashews are a surprising and tasty addition to the batter.

YIELD | 10 SERVINGS

1	cup all-purpose flour + more for dusting	½	cup milk
⅔	cup oat flakes	½	cup honey
1	tablespoon baking powder	⅓	cup safflower or canola oil
2	large eggs, lightly beaten	½	cup raisins
½	cup whole-milk plain yogurt	½	cup chopped unsalted cashews

Preheat the oven to 350°F. Lightly butter and flour a 9-by-5-inch loaf pan.

In a medium bowl, using a fork, stir together the 1 cup flour, oat flakes, and baking powder.

In a large bowl, beat together the eggs, yogurt, milk, honey, and oil. Stir in the flour mixture, raisins, and cashews. Pour the batter into the prepared pan and level with a rubber spatula.

Bake in the center of the oven until a cake tester comes out clean, 50 to 60 minutes. Let cool in the pan for 10 minutes and then on a cake rack until completely cool.

EASY OLIVE BREAD

This bread is delicious on its own, or you can serve it sliced, toasted, and spread with a little garlic butter.

YIELD | 10 SERVINGS

1	cup all-purpose flour + more for dusting
1	cup whole wheat flour
1	tablespoon baking powder
1	teaspoon sea salt
2	tablespoons unsalted butter, melted
1	tablespoon olive oil + more for greasing
1	extra-large egg, lightly beaten
½	teaspoon dried rosemary
2	teaspoons grated lemon zest (see page 262)
½	teaspoon Aleppo pepper or crushed red pepper flakes
1	cup milk
1¼	cups black oil-cured or kalamata olives, pitted and coarsely chopped

Preheat the oven to 350°F. Lightly oil and flour a 9-by-5-inch loaf pan.

In a medium bowl, stir together the 1 cup all-purpose flour, whole wheat flour, baking powder, and salt.

In a large bowl, beat together the butter, the 1 tablespoon oil, egg, rosemary, lemon zest, and pepper or red pepper flakes. Stir in the flour mixture, alternating with the milk and beating after each addition. Fold in the olives. Pour into the prepared pan.

Bake until a cake tester comes out clean, about 1 hour. Let cool in the pan for 10 minutes, then remove the bread from the pan and let cool completely on a cake rack.

ROSEMARY FOCACCIA

A distant cousin of pizza, this satisfying bread will soon be added to your can-do baking skills. Feel free to make it your own by changing the topping and adding or substituting pitted sliced olives, basil, minced oil-cured sun-dried tomatoes, or peppers. You can sprinkle it with finely grated cheese just when it comes out of the oven. You can even make it with no topping at all; just brush with a little olive oil and sprinkle on a little salt before baking. But don't call it "focach"—three syllables, please.

YIELD | 12 SERVINGS

Bread

1	packet (¼ ounce) active dry yeast		1	cup room-temperature milk
1	teaspoon sugar		1	cup room-temperature water
½	cup warm water		3	tablespoons extra-virgin olive oil + more for greasing
5–6	cups bread flour			
1	teaspoon sea salt			
1	tablespoon chopped fresh rosemary			

Topping

3	tablespoons extra-virgin olive oil		2	tablespoons chopped fresh rosemary
1	medium–large red onion, sliced			
6	cloves garlic, sliced		1–2	teaspoons coarse salt

Lightly coat a 17-by-14-inch baking sheet with olive oil. Coat a ceramic bowl with olive oil.

To make the bread: In a large bowl, dissolve the yeast and sugar in the warm water. Stir and let stand until bubbly, about 5 minutes. Stir in 1 cup of the flour, salt, and rosemary. Let rest for 5 minutes.

In a medium pouring bowl, mix the milk, room-temperature water, and the oil.

With a wooden spoon or the paddle attachment of a stand mixer set on low, alternately beat the milk mixture and the remaining 4 to 5 cups flour by the cup into the yeast mixture. When the dough starts to hold together, place on a lightly floured surface and knead until smooth and elastic, about 5 minutes.

(continued)

Place the dough in the prepared ceramic bowl. Rotate the dough so that it is coated in oil and cover the bowl with a clean, damp kitchen towel. Let stand for 2 hours, or until more or less doubled in volume. Gently deflate the dough in the bowl, turn it over, and let rise for another 45 minutes.

To make the topping: Heat the oil in a heavy skillet over medium-low heat. Add the onion and cook for 10 minutes, then add the garlic and cook until the onions are caramelized, another 2 minutes. Remove from the heat and let come to room temperature. With a slotted spoon, remove the onion and garlic to a small bowl. Reserve the oil in the skillet.

Preheat the oven to 400°F.

To assemble the focaccia: Stretch the dough into a 16-by-13-inch rectangle on a lightly floured surface. Cover and let rest for 30 minutes. Place on the prepared baking sheet and stretch gently to fit. With your fingertips, dimple the top of the dough, making indentations about 1½ inches apart and ¼ inch deep. Brush with the reserved olive oil and spread the onion and garlic over all. Sprinkle with the rosemary and coarse salt.

Bake until the edges are golden brown, about 30 minutes. Let cool on a rack for 15 to 20 minutes before serving.

If you must prepare ahead of time, let the cooked bread cool thoroughly, cover with plastic wrap and foil, and refrigerate for up to 24 hours. Remove all the wrapping and heat in a 350°F oven for 5 to 7 minutes.

EASY WHOLE WHEAT BREAD

YIELD | 10 SERVINGS

1	large potato, peeled and diced	2	packages (½ ounce) active dry yeast
2	tablespoons unsalted butter + more for greasing	3	cups whole wheat flour or a multigrain mixture
¼	cup honey	¼	teaspoon salt
¼	cup warm water		

Generously butter a 9-by-5-inch loaf pan.

Bring 1½ cups water to a low boil and simmer the potato for 20 minutes, or until it falls apart at the touch of a fork. Strain the water through a fine-mesh strainer into a heatproof measuring cup and add the 2 tablespoons butter. Set aside the potato water.

Meanwhile, in a small bowl, stir the honey into the water until dissolved. Add the yeast, stir once or twice, and let stand until bubbly, about 5 minutes.

Place the flour in a large bowl and make a well in the center. Pour the yeast mixture into the center, cover with a towel, and allow to foam for 10 minutes. Add the potato water to the center of the flour and sprinkle the salt over all. Allow to foam for 20 minutes.

With a rubber spatula, work the flour from the center and thoroughly incorporate all the ingredients. Cover the bowl with a clean, damp kitchen towel and let rise until doubled, about 2 hours.

Turn out the dough onto a lightly floured surface and knead until smooth and elastic, about 10 minutes. Shape into a loaf and place in the prepared pan. Cover with a damp kitchen towel and let rise until doubled in the pan.

Preheat the oven to 400°F.

Bake in the center of the oven for 45 minutes. Let cool in the pan for 15 minutes, then turn out onto a cake rack to cool thoroughly.

TIPS FOR POTLUCKING

These days, luck plays only a small part in most of our gatherings—and sometimes there is not a pot in sight. But any time people get together, and some or all of them bring food to eat together, it's a potluck. It would seem from my travels that is the way America is eating today, and we are enjoying every moment of it. My favorite quote from a host is: "We like to eat. We especially like to eat good food. But we really, *really* like to eat good food with each other."

Dinner parties and small buffets tend to be very organized but sometimes, large events take on a life of their own. For example, I remember attending a very Happy New Year's party where we had everything from sushi to potato pancakes.

Whether your potluck is large or small, the following tips can help make your event a success.

The first three tips are: Communicate. Communicate. Communicate.

HOSTING

It is important to understand that even though you are hosting, you won't have total control. However, hosting the event is your main task. Your hospitality and generosity in opening your home (or establishing a special location) is a huge contribution and very rewarding. Think of it as taking the pressure off your guests to make a lot of decisions. Usually 2 to 3 weeks is enough of a heads-up for something simple; for a special event, you might want to start planning 1 to 2 months ahead.

The secret to success is organizing. Start with phone calls or emails to the people you think that you can count on and tell them what you have in mind. If someone on your list says that they don't think they can prepare anything, for whatever reason, never, *never* uninvite them. Suggest that perhaps they can bring a loaf of really great bread or just the pleasure of their company.

Whether you're the host or the guest at the next potluck, look through this book and see what strikes your fancy. The recipes are, as promised, classic crowd-pleasers. You might want to buddy up with one or more people who are invited and collaborate so that each of you makes something from a different chapter.

BY THE NUMBERS

Menu planning works something like this. If you are having 10 to 12 people at a potluck, you will want two or three appetizers, one main dish, two sides, a salad, good bread and butter (or extra-virgin olive oil for dipping), condiments, two desserts, and beverages. If the number of guests is doubled, simply have three or four appetizers, double the volume of the main dish or have two or three different choices, three sides, a large salad, and three desserts, along with the other elements of the meal. Sometimes there will be a guest who always likes to make salad or dessert. That's fine. Work with it. If there are too many offers for the same dish just politely say, "We already have three pasta salads. Please bring that delicious soup you make." Don't be too rigid. You can ask for a specific course but then see what people want to make. It's supposed to be fun.

When you are hosting ask people to bring food as finished and ready-to-serve as possible. Double check what guests need in the way of stove-top or oven use, refrigerator or freezer space. Do they need electric outlets? Will a heavy-duty extension cord be necessary? Let people know what to expect. Ask them if they are bringing food in or with a serving dish and inquire about any special utensils and condiments that may be needed. And don't forget ice. Often a large Styrofoam cooler will hold enough ice for a single event.

SERVING STATIONS AND TABLE SET-UP

If it's possible, set up "stations" as the pros do. One table, credenza, or buffet top for appetizers; one surface for the main portion of the meal; and another for coffee and dessert will go a long way to present your potluck choices at their best. A teacart or a folding table makes a nice bar and will minimize spills. One friend in a small apartment uses a sturdy ironing board as a serving table and covers it with a tablecloth over plastic. I used to be averse to those little TV tables, but they can come in very handy when you want to eat and drink at the same time.

PLEASE BE SEATED

If you want everyone seated at the same table and you don't have one with many leaves, you can make a T out of two tables. You can also rent a 72-inch folding table if you have the room and the budget for it. This size seats 10 to 12 comfortably. Some places will even rent just a tabletop that you can set on your own table to enlarge it. A friend rents three 4-foot tables for her parties; the rental fee is $25 for all three tables. The upside of rental: You don't have to worry about storing unwieldy tables between events! In addition, that assortment of folding chairs most of us have acquired look great with washable slipcovers that give them a clean and comfortable look. Of course, your choice depends entirely on the size of your home and your inclination.

MAKING ROOM

If you are hosting an event where you expect guests to mingle, clear furniture surfaces in the room where guests will be eating and drinking. It may look sparse before your guests arrive, but everyone will appreciate having a place to set down a plate or glass. Whatever you decide, remember that most people are thrilled to be out and about sharing good food and good company, and they're not worried about how you set up your dining area.

POTLUCK SERVING SIZES

Each recipe in this book lists the serving portions and amounts, and most of these recipes were created to serve 8 to 12 people. Before scaling up or scaling down a recipe, it's best to first cook (or bake) it as written. If you need a greater quantity for your potluck, I'd suggest making the recipe in two batches, rather than doubling it. That way, you won't have to adjust pan sizes and oven temperatures. However, many of these recipes can be easily doubled or halved to suit your crowd. If you double the recipe but don't really need as many as 20 to 24 portions, check the recipe to see if the remainder can be frozen for a later meal.

Potlucks offer an opportunity to taste and enjoy a sampling of many flavors. The larger the group, the more forgiving the menu. Guests will appreciate the two lasagnas and the two apple pies (and they were probably made with very different recipes). Everyone understands that if one dish is already empty on this end of the table, there's another dish over there that looks just as delicious. If more than 10 to 20 people are expected at an event, the serving size of each dish does not have to equal the number of guests, unless of course you volunteered to provide that amount.

TRY YOUR LUCK

I suggest that you ignore the old saw about not cooking something new when you are presenting food to others. What better time to expand your repertoire or elaborate on an old favorite! Since you are usually making only one dish for a potluck, stretch your skills a bit and try Fillet of Fish en Papillotte (page 135) or Tiramisu (page 179). That being said, if you have never made a pie before and are worried about rolling out piecrust, it might be better to give the recipe a whirl a week or two before the event. For most dishes, though, if you think you can do it—you probably can.

GATHER YOUR INGREDIENTS

Read the recipe thoroughly before you go shopping. Make a list of ingredients that you may need to buy and check that you have the pans and tools needed. You can often improvise, but you don't want the crust rolled and the oven hot only to find out that your pie pan is not 10 inches across.

TAKING YOUR DISH ALONG

If you're traveling to a potluck, be sure to decide ahead of time how you will transport the dish. To keep cold food cold and hot food hot, refrigerate food before putting it into a cooled insulated container or heat food before putting it into a warmed thermal carrier. Cold gel packs are an inexpensive and effective coolant. You can also buy hot packs that can be heated in a microwave or regular oven. If you have the room to store them, inexpensive Styrofoam chests are very handy for cold or hot food. There are also insulated, soft-sided thermal carriers that zip closed and are very effective in keeping foods cold or hot.

FRESH FROM SCRATCH

Virtually all the recipes in this book call for fresh ingredients. These days, with few exceptions, supermarkets and specialty stores have abundant choices. And many, with a week or so notice, will get you what you want. Amazing! You can, of course, successfully make some substitutions. At the end of the day, once you get used to a mainly "from scratch" kitchen, you will find cooking actually much easier and more rewarding.

Meat, poultry, fish and shellfish are best used fresh, rather than frozen, especially if you are going to freeze the dish you are making. If you do use these ingredients frozen, thaw them completely before cooking.

- I would request that no substitutes be made for fresh lemon, lime, or orange juice or the zest of their fruits. Artificial or processed citrus flavors always seem to give a chemical taste to dishes prepared with them.
- Garlic has some of the same issues. There really is no substitute for fresh garlic. It should almost never be served raw; if it is, discard the central green stem in each clove and thoroughly smash the clove. Pure garlic powder will give you the closest taste. Other forms are less dependable.
- To put it bluntly, I never use margarine because I don't like it. If you want to substitute margarine for butter for dietary reasons, it will often work.
- If a vegetable or a berry is out of season, you can substitute frozen for fresh. Canned foods, with the exception of tomatoes and beans, aren't as good.
- As far as salads go, try to avoid packaged mixed greens. They simply don't have the flavorful crunch you get from 2 or 3 heads of lettuce. Single-item packages, such as baby spinach or arugula, seem more appetizing.
- Try to use fresh herbs and whole spices that you mince or crush as needed for a recipe. To substitute dried herbs for fresh, use about ⅓ the amount of the dried. When you buy spices, put the date on them so that you know when they are no longer at their peak. Ground spices are good for about a year and whole spices for two.
- It is better to fill your own spray bottle with the oil of your choice than to use commercially prepared bottles, which have chemical propellants that eventually ruin the surface of your cookware.

SPECIAL DIETARY NEEDS

There are endless opinions about individual allergies, distastes, and dietary preferences. My position is that it is the responsibility of any adult with food concerns to honor them by taking charge of what they need to eat and not expect to a group meal to comply with their special needs. For instance, though the host should indicate the presence of peanuts, the person with the allergy should inquire. The same is true of shellfish or wheat or dairy products. If you are hosting, never push anyone to eat anything they don't want to. On the other hand, if you are a guest, ask before eating a dish that may not be good for you and set aside for yourself a good portion of the dish that you prepared.

A WORD ABOUT KITCHEN CLEANLINESS

Once a month, clean out your refrigerator. Throw away everything that's past its prime, especially "mystery" containers. The adage is "When in doubt, throw it out." Don't taste or ask anyone else to taste food you think is *off.* This will free up space to store a stew overnight or to chill bowls of cookie dough.

Use hot, soapy water. Wash your hands, utensils, equipment, and work surfaces thoroughly in hot, soapy water for 30 seconds before and after you come into contact with any food. Rinse equipment well and dry with paper towels or kitchen towels.

Take care not to contaminate. Don't cross-contaminate by letting bacteria spread from one food product to another. Keep raw meat, poultry, and seafood away from ready-to-eat foods. If you have drained a marinade from raw food, do not use it as is. You may continue basting whatever you are cooking, or bring it to a boil if you want to use it as a base for sauce. Never place cooked food on the same plate that was used for raw food without washing the plate first.

Call if you have questions. The USDA has great toll-free resources for consumers with food safety questions. Call the USDA Meat and Poultry Hotline at (888) 674-6854 or email at www.fsis.usda.gov. The hotline is available in English and Spanish and can be reached from 10:00 a.m. to 4:00 p.m. (Eastern Time) on weekdays.

USEFUL KITCHEN HINTS

These culinary tips will help you prepare some of the recipes in *Classic Potluck Dishes.*

HEAT SETTINGS

- High heat is for boiling only.
- Medium to medium-high heat is for sautéing and frying.

- Medium-low heat is for heating and keeping food hot.
- Low heat is for simmering and preparing sauces.

If you're using an electric range and need to move a pot from high to medium or low, it is better to have a second burner ready to go at the lower temperature, rather than waiting for the electric burner to cool down.

ROASTING GARLIC

To roast garlic whole, remove the outermost papery skins. Cut about ½-inch from the top of the head, trimming just enough to expose the tips of the garlic cloves. Place the garlic, root end down, in a baking dish or on foil and generously drizzle olive oil over the head. Cover tightly with foil and bake at 325°F until tender, about 45 minutes to 1 hour.

TOASTING COCONUT

Preheat the oven to 325°F. Place the shredded coconut in a single layer on a baking sheet, breaking up any clumps. Bake for about 7 to 10 minutes until golden brown. Every 2 to 3 minutes turn the coconut with a spatula so that it browns evenly. The coconut will crisp a bit as it browns. Remove the baking sheet from the oven and transfer the coconut to a cool baking sheet to stop the cooking.

MAKING CITRUS ZEST

The zest of citrus fruit is the thin, brightly colored portion of the outer peel; it's rich in flavorful oils and is used to infuse sauces and garnishes. For slivers of zest, use a citrus zester, vegetable peeler, or a sharp paring knife to remove strips of zest, taking care not to peel into the bitter white pith. Go slowly when peeling to create continuous strips of zest.

To grate zest, use a multisided grater or Microplane grater and rub the fruit back and forth; work over a plate to catch the grated zest. Rotate the fruit as you work, making sure that you do not remove the bitter white pith (or membrane) just underneath the peel. Be careful not to cut your fingertips when zesting because graters can be very sharp.

CLARIFIED BUTTER

This traditional cooking ingredient predates refrigeration. These days, it is best to store it in the refrigerator for up to 3 to 4 weeks. Slice 1 pound (4 sticks) of unsalted butter and place it in a small, heavy saucepan over medium-low heat. When the butter melts and starts to foam, lower the heat. Do not stir. Remove from the heat after five minutes when the surface is covered with foam. Skim off the foam and discard. You will see clear butter separated from the milk solids. Strain the clear butter into a clean glass jar or container (plastic is not recommended) that has a tight cover. Cool, cover, and refrigerate. Use clarified butter in recipes when it's called for and for sautéing; it has a higher burning point and a more delicate taste than whole butter.

THE SCOVILLE SCALE

Developed by chemist Water Scoville in 1912, the Scoville Scale was developed to measure the "heat" in chili peppers. The higher the number of Scoville units, the hotter the pepper. Peppers contain capsaicin, and the Scoville Scale measures the amount of capsaicin in various peppers. Bell or sweet peppers do not contain measurable amounts of capsaicin so they score zero on the scale. Habenero peppers, on the other hand, have a rating of 300,000 or more.

THE SCOVILLE SCALE	
Pepper	**Scoville Rating**
Bell pepper	0
Pepperoncini	100–500
Anaheim pepper	500–1000
Poblano pepper	1,000–1,500
Jalapeño pepper	2,500–8,000
Chipotle pepper	2,500–10,000
Wax pepper	5,000–10,000
Serrano pepper	10,000–23,000
Cayenne pepper	30,000–50,000
Thai pepper	50,000–100,000
Habenero pepper	100,000–350,000

INDEX

Underscored page references indicate sidebar notes. **Boldfaced** page references indicate photographs.